THE UNFORTUNATE TRAVELLER OR THE LIFE OF JACK WILTON

BY THOMAS NASH

AN ESSAY ON THE LIFE AND WRITINGS OF THOMAS NASH.

It is mainly, no doubt, but I hope not exclusively, an antiquarian interest which attaches to the name of Thomas Nash. It would be absurd to claim for a writer so obscure a very prominent place in the procession of Englishmen of letters. His works proclaim by their extreme rarity the fact that three centuries of readers have existed cheerfully and wholesomely without any acquaintance with their contents. At the present moment, the number of those living persons who have actually perused the works of Nash may probably be counted on the fingers of two hands. Most of these productions are uncommon to excess, one or two exist in positively unique examples. There is no use in arguing against such a fact as this. If Nash had reached, or even approached, the highest order of merit, he would have been placed, long ere this, within the reach of all. Nevertheless, his merits, relative if not positive, were great. In the violent coming of age of Elizabethan literature, his voice was heard loudly, not always discordantly, and with an accent eminently personal to himself. His life, though shadowy, has elements of picturesqueness and pathos; his writings are a storehouse of oddity and fantastic wit

It has been usual to class Nash with the Precursors of Shakespeare, and until quite lately it was conjectured that he was older than Greene and Peele, a contemporary of Lodge and Chapman. It is now known that he was considerably younger than all these, and even than Marlowe and Shakespeare. Thomas Nash, the fourth child of the Rev. William Nash, who to have been curate of Lowestoft in Suffolk, was baptized in that town in November, 1567. The Nashes continued to live in Lowestoft, where the father died in 1603, probably three years after the death of his son Thomas. Of the latter we hear nothing more until, in October, 1582, at the age of fifteen, he matriculated as a sizar of St. John's College, Cambridge. Cooper says that he was admitted a scholar on the Lady Margaret's foundation in 1584. He remained at Cambridge, in unbroken residence, until July, 1589, "seven year together, lacking a quarter," as he tells us positively in "Lenten Stuff."

Cambridge was the hotbed of all that was vivid and revolutionary in literature at that moment, and Robert Greene was the centre of literary Cambridge. When Nash arrived, Greene, who was seven years his senior, was still in residence at his study in Clare Hall, having returned from his travels in Italy and Spain, ready, in 1583, to take his degree as master of arts. He was soon, however, to leave for London, and it is unlikely that a boy of sixteen would be immediately admitted to the society of those "lewd wags" who looked up to the already distinguished Greene as to a master. But Greene, without doubt, made frequent visits to his university, and on one of these was probably formed that intimate friendship with Nash which lasted until near the elder poet's death. Marlowe was at Corpus, then called Benet College, during five years of Nash's residence, but it is by no means certain that their acquaintance began so early. It is, indeed, in the highest degree tantalizing that these writers, many of whom loved nothing better than to talk about themselves, should have neglected to give us the information which would precisely be most welcome to us. A dozen whole "Anatomies of Absurdity" and "Supplications of Pierce Penniless" might be eagerly exchanged for a few pages in which the literary life of Cambridge from 1582 to 1589 should be frankly and definitely described.

It has been surmised that Nash was ejected from the university in 1587. His enemy, Gabriel Harvey, who was extremely ill-informed, gives this account of what occurred:—

"[At Cambridge], (being distracted of his wits) [Nash] fell into diverse misdemeanours, which were the first steps that brought him to this poor estate. As, namely, in his fresh-time, how he flourished in all impudency towards scholars, and abuse to the townsmen; insomuch that to this day the townsmen call every untoward scholar of whom there is great hope, *a very Nash*. Then, being bachelor of arts, which by great labour he got, to show afterwards that he was not unworthy of it, had a hand in a show called *Terminus et non terminus*; for the which his partner in it was expelled the college; but this foresaid Nash played in it (as I suppose) the Varlet of Clubs.... Then suspecting himself that he should be stayed for *egregie dunsus*, and not attain to the next degree, said he had commenced enough, and so forsook Cambridge, being bachelor of the third year."

But, even in this poor gossip, we find nothing about ejection. Nash's extraordinary abuse of language is probably the cause of that report. In 1589, in prefacing his "Anatomy of Absurdity," he remarked:—

"What I have written proceeded not from the pen of vainglory, but from the process of that pensiveness, which two summers since overtook me; whose obscured cause, best known to every name of curse, hath compelled my wit to wander abroad unregarded in this satirical disguise, and counselled my content to dislodge his delight from traitors' eyes."

That the young gentleman meant something by these sentences, it is only charitable to suppose; that he could have been intelligible, even to his immediate contemporaries, is hardly to be believed. This "obscured cause" has been taken to be, by some, his removal from the University, and, by others, his entanglement with a young woman. It is perhaps simpler to understand him to say that the ensuing pamphlet was written, in consequence of an intellectual crisis, in 1587, when he was twenty years of age.

At twenty-two, at all events, we find him in London, beginning his career as a man of letters. His first separate publication seems to have been the small quarto in black letter from which a quotation has just been made. This composition, named an "Anatomy" in imitation of several then recent popular treatises of a similar title, is only to be pardoned on the supposition that it was a boyish manuscript prepared at college. It is vilely written, in the preposterous Euphuism of the moment; the style is founded on Lyly, the manner is the manner of Greene, and Whetstone in his moral "Mirrors" and "Heptamerons" has supplied the matter. The "absurdity" satirized in this jejune and tedious tract is extravagant living of all kinds. The author attacks women with great vehemence, but only in that temper which permitted the young Juvenals of the hour to preach against wine and cards and stageplays with intense zeal, while practising the worship of all these with equal ardour. "The Anatomy of Absurdity" is a purely academic exercise, interesting only because it shows, in the praise of Sidney and the passage in defence of poetry, something of the intellectual aptitude of the youthful writer.

In the same year, and a little earlier, Nash published an address "to the gentlemen students of both universities," as a preface to a romance by Greene. Bibliographers describe a supposititious "Menaphon" of 1587, which nobody has ever seen; even if such an edition existed, it is certain that Nash's address was not prefixed to it, for the style is greatly in advance of his boyish writing of that year. It is an interesting document, enthusiastic and gay in a manner hardly to be met with again in its author, and diversified with graceful praise of St John's College, defence of good poetry, and wholesome ridicule of those who were trying to introduce the "Thrasonical huffsnuff" style of which Phaer and Stanihurst were the prophets.

Still in 1589, but later in the year, Nash is believed to have thrown himself into that extraordinary clash of theological weapons which is celebrated as the Martin Marprelate Controversy. As is well known, this pamphlet war grew out of the passionate resentment felt by the Puritans against the tyrannical acts of Whitgift and the Bishops. The actual controversy has been traced back to a defence of the establishment of the Church, by the Dean of Sarum, on the one hand, and a treatise by John Penry the Puritan, on the other, both published in 1587. In 1588 followed the violent Puritan libel, called "Martin Marprelate," secretly printed, and written, perhaps, by a lawyer named Barrow. Towards the close of the dispute several of the literary wits dashed in upon the prelatical side, and denounced the Martinists with exuberant high spirits. Among these Nash was long thought to have held a very prominent place, for the two most brilliant tracts of the entire controversy, "Pap with an Hatchet," 1589, and "An Almond for a Parrot," 1590, were confidently attributed to him. These are now, however, clearly perceived to be the work of a much riper pen, that, namely, of Lyly.

It is probable that the four anonymous and privately printed tracts, which Dr. Grosart has finally selected, do represent Nash's share in the Marprelate Controversy, although in one of them, "Martin's Month's Mind," I cannot say that I recognize his manner. The "Countercuff," published in August, 1589, from Gravesend, shows a great advance in power. The academic Euphuism has been laid aside; images and trains of thought are taken from life and experience instead of from books. In "Pasquils Return," which belongs to October of the same year, the author invents the happy word "Pruritans" to annoy his enemy, and speaks, probably in his own name, but perhaps in that of Pasquil, of a visit to Antwerp. "Martin's Month's Mind," which is a crazy piece of fustian, belongs to December, 1589, while the fourth tract, "Pasquil's Apology," appeared so late as July, 1590. The smart and active pen which skirmishes in these pamphlets adds nothing serious to the consideration of the tragical controversy in which it so lightly took part. It amused and trained Nash to write these satires, but they left Udall none the worse and the Bishops none the better. The author repeatedly promises to rehearse the arguments on both sides and sum up the entire controversy in a "May-Game of Martinism," of which we hear no more.

During the first twelve months of Nash's residence in London he was pretty busily employed. It is just conceivable that six small publications may have brought in money enough to support him. But after this we perceive no obvious source of income for some considerable time. How the son of a poor Suffolk minister contrived to live in London throughout the years 1590 and 1591, it is difficult to imagine. Certainly not on the proceeds of a single pamphlet. It is not credible that Nash published much that has not come down to us. Perhaps a tract here and there may have been lost.{1} He probably subsisted by hanging on to the outskirts of education. Perhaps he taught pupils, more likely still he wrote letters. We know, afterall, too little of the manners of the age to venture on a reply to the question which constantly imposes itself, How did the minor Elizabethan man of letters earn a livelihood? In the case of Nash, I would hazard the conjecture, which is borne out, I think, by several allusions in his writings, that he was a reader to the press, connected, perhaps, with the Queen's printers, or with those under the special protection of the Bishops.

1 One long narrative poem, the very name of which is too   coarse to quote, was, according to Oldys, certainly   published; but of this no printed copy is known to exist.   John Davies of Hereford says that "good men tore that   pamphlet to pieces." I owe to the kindness of Mr. A. H.   Bullen the inspection of a transcript of a very corrupt   manuscript of this work.

His only production in 1591, so far as we know, was the insignificant tract called "A Wonderful Astrological Prognostication," by "Adam Fouleweather." This has been hastily treated as a defence of "the dishonoured memory" of Nash's dead friend Greene against Gabriel Harvey. But Greene did not die till the end of 1592, and in the "Prognostication" there is nothing about either Greene or Harvey. The pamphlet is a quizzical satire on the almanac-makers, very much in the spirit of Swift's Bickerstaff "Predictions" a hundred years later. Of more importance was a preface contributed in this same year to Sir Philip Sidney's posthumous "Astrophel and Stella." In this short essay Nash reaches a higher level of eloquence than he had yet achieved, and, in spite of its otiose redundancy, this enthusiastic eulogy of Sidney is pleasant reading.

In 1592, doubtless prior to the death of Greene, Nash published the earliest of his important books, the volume entitled "Pierce Penniless his Supplication to the Devil." This is a grotesque satire on the vices and the eccentricities of the age. As a specimen of prose style it is remarkable for its spirit and "go," qualities which may enable us to forget how turbid, ungraceful, and harsh it is. Nash had now dropped the mannerism of the Euphuists; he had hardly gained a style of his own. "Pierce Penniless," with its chains of "letter-leaping metaphors," rattles breathlessly on, and at length abruptly ceases. Any sense of the artistic fashioning of a sentence, or of the relative harmony of the parts of a composition, was not yet dreamed of. But before we condemn the muddy turbulence of the author, we must recollect that nothing had then been published of Hooker, Raleigh, or Bacon in the pedestrian manner. Genuine English prose had begun to exist indeed, but had not yet been revealed to the world. Nash, as a lively portrait-painter in grotesque, at this time, is seen at his best in such a caricature as this, scourging "the pride of the Dane":—

"The most gross and senseless proud dolts are the Danes, who stand so much upon their unwieldy burly-boned soldiery, that they account of no man that hath not a battle-axe at his girdle to hough dogs with, or wears not a cock's feather in a thrummed hat like a cavalier. Briefly, he is the best fool braggart under heaven. For besides nature hath lent him a flab-berkin face, like one of the four winds, and cheeks that sag like a woman's dug over his chinbone, his apparel is so stuffed up with bladders of taffaty, and his back like beef stuffed with parsley, so drawn out with ribbands and devises, and blistered with light sarcenet bastings, that you would think him nothing but a swarm of butterflies, if you saw him afar off."

On the 3rd of September, 1592, Greene came to his miserable end, having sent to the press from his deathbed those two remarkable pamphlets, the "Groatsworth of Wit" and the "Repentance." For two years past, if we may believe Nash, the profligate atheism of the elder poet had estranged his friend, or at all events had kept him at a distance. But a feeling of common loyalty, and the anger which a true man of letters feels when a genuine poet is traduced by a pedant, led Nash to take up a very strong position as a defender of the reputation of Greene. Gabriel Harvey, although the friend of Spenser, is a personage who fills an odious place in the literary history of the last years of Elizabeth. He was a scholar and a university man of considerable attainments, but he was wholly without taste, and he concentrated into vinegar a temper which must always have had a tendency to be sour. In particular, he loathed the school of young writers who had become famous in direct opposition to the literary laws which he had laid down.

Harvey's wrath had found a definite excuse in the tract, called "A Quip for an upstart Courtier, or a quaint dispute between Velvet-Breeches and Cloth-Breeches," which Greene had published early in the year 1592. Accordingly, when he heard of Greene's death, he hastened to his lodgings, interviewed his landlady, collected scurrilous details, and, with matchless bad taste, issued, before the month was over, his "Four Letters," a pamphlet in which he trampled upon the memory of Greene. In the latest of his public utterances, Greene had made an appeal to three friends, who, though not actually named, are understood to have been Marlowe, Peele, and Nash.

Of these, the last was the one with the readiest pen, and the task of punishing Harvey fell upon him.

Nash's first attack on Harvey took the form of a small volume, entitled, "Strange News of the Intercepting of Certain Letters," published very early in 1593. It was a close confutation of the charges made in Harvey's "Four Letters," the vulgarity and insolence of the pedant being pressed home with an insistence which must have been particularly galling to him as coming from a distinguished man of his own university, twenty years his junior. Harvey retorted with the heavy artillery of his "Pierce's Supererogation," which was mainly directed against Nash, whom the disappearance of Peele, and the sudden death of Marlowe in June, had left without any very intimate friend as a supporter. Nash retired, for the moment, from the controversy, and in the prefatory epistle to a remarkable work, the most bulky of all his books, "Christ's Tears over Jerusalem," he waved the white flag. He bade, he declared, "a hundred unfortunate farewells to fantastical satirism," and complimented his late antagonist on his "abundant scholarship." Harvey took no notice of this, and for four years their mutual animosity slumbered. In this same year, 1593, Nash produced the only play which has come down to us as wholly composed by him, the comedy of "Summer's Last Will and Testament."

Meanwhile "Pierce Penniless" had enjoyed a remarkable success, and had placed Nash in a prominent position among London men of letters. We learn that in 1596, four years after its original publication, it had run through six editions, besides being translated in 1594 into French, and, a little later, into Macaronic Latin. In "Christ's Tears" the young writer, conscious of his new importance, deals with what the critics have said about his style. He tells us, and we cannot wonder at it, that objections have been made to "my boisterous compound words, and ending my Italianate coined verbs all in *ize*." His defence is not unlike that of De Quincey; we can imagine his asking, when urged to be simple, whether simplicity be in place in a description of Belshazzar's Feast He says that the Saxon monosyllables that swarm in the English tongue are a scandal to it, and that he is only turning this cheap silver trash into fine gold coinage. Books, he says, written in plain English, "seem like shopkeepers' boxes, that contain nothing else save halfpence, three-farthings, and two-pences." To show what sort of doubloons he proposes to mint for English pockets, we need go no further than the opening phrases of his dedication of this very book to that amiable poet, the Lady Elizabeth Carey:—

"Excellent accomplished court-glorifying Lady, give me leave, with the sportive sea-porpoises, preludiately a little to play before the storm of my tears, to make my prayer before

I proceed to my sacrifice. Lo, for an oblation to the rich burnished shrine of your virtue, a handful of Jerusalem's mummianized earth, in a few sheets of waste paper enwrapped, I here, humiliate, offer up at your feet."

These, however, in spite of the odd neologisms, are sentences formed in a novel and a greatly improved manner, and the improvement is sustained throughout this curious volume. Probably the intimate study of the Authorized Version of the Bible, which this semi-theological tractate necessitated, had much to do with the clarification of the author's style. At all events, from this time forth, Nash drops, except in polemical passages where his design is provocative, that irritating harshness in volubility which had hitherto marked his manner of writing. Here, for example, is a passage from "Christ's Tears" which is not without a strangely impressive melody:—

"Over the Temple, at the solemn feast of the Passover, was seen a comet most coruscant, streamed and tailed forth, with glistering naked swords, which in his mouth, as a man in his hand all at once, he made semblance as if he shaked and vambrashed. Seven days it continued; all which time, the Temple was as clear and light in the night as it had been noonday. In the Sanctum Sanctorum was heard clashing and hewing of armour, while flocks of ravens, with a fearful croaking cry, beat, fluttered and clashed against the windows. A hideous dismal owl, exceeding all her kind in deformity and quantity, in the Temple-porch built her nest. From under the altar there issued penetrating plangorous howlings and ghastly deadmen's groans."

He tells us, in the preface, that he takes an autumnal air, and in truth there is a melancholy refinement in this volume which we may seek for in vain elsewhere in Nash's writings. The greater part of the book is a "collachrimate oration" over Jerusalem, placed in the mouth of our Saviour; by degrees the veil of Jerusalem grows thinner and thinner, and we see more and more clearly through it the London of Elizabeth, denounced by a pensive and not, this time, a turbulent satirist.

In 1594 Nash's pen was particularly active. It was to the Lady Elizabeth Carey, again, that he dedicated "The Terrors of the Night," a discourse on apparitions. He describes some very agreeable ghosts, as, for instance, those which appeared to a gentleman, a friend of the author's, in the guise of "an inveigling troop of naked virgins, whose odoriferous breath more perfumed the air than ordnance would that is charged with amomum, musk, civet and ambergreece." It was surely a mock-modesty which led Nash to fear that such ghost-stories as these would appear to his readers duller than Holland cheese and more tiresome than homespun. To 1594, too, belongs the tragedy of "Dido," probably left incomplete by Marlowe, and finished by Nash, who shows himself here an adept in that swelling bombast of bragging blank verse of which he affected to disapprove. A new edition of "Christ's Tears" also belongs to this busy year 1594, which however is mainly interesting to us as having seen the publication of the work which we are here introducing to modern readers.

An eminent French critic, M. Jusserand, whose knowledge of English sixteenth-century literature is unsurpassed, was the first to draw attention to the singular interest which attaches to "The Unfortunate Traveller, or the Life of Jack Wilton," 1594. In his treatise, "Le Roman au Temps de Shakespeare," 1887, M. Jusserand insisted upon the fact that this neglected book was the best specimen of the *picaresque* tale written in English before the days of Defoe. He shows that expressions put in the mouth of Nash's hero, which had been carelessly treated as autobiographical confessions of foreign travel and the like, on the part of the author, were but features of a carefully planned fiction. "Jack Wilton" describes the career of an adventurer, from his early youth as a page in the royal camp of Henry VIII. at the siege of Tournay, to his attainment of wealth, position, and a beautiful Italian wife.

The first exploit of the page is an encounter with a fraudulent innkeeper, which is described with great spirit, and M. Jusserand has ingeniously surmised that Shakespeare, after reading these pages, determined to fuse the two characters, mine host and the waggish picaroon, into the single immortal figure of Falstaff. After this point in the tale, it is probable that the reader may find the interest of the story flag; but his attention will be reawakened when he reaches the episode of the Earl of Surrey and Fair Geraldine, and that in which Jack, pretending to be Surrey, runs off with his sweet Venetian mistress, Diamante. It will be for the reader of the ensuing pages to say whether Nash had mastered the art of narrative

5

quite so perfectly as M. Jusserand, in his just pride as a discoverer, seems to think. The romance, no doubt, is incoherent and languid at times, and is easily led aside into channels of gorgeous description and vain moral reflection.

It will doubtless be of interest, at this point, to quote the words in which, in a later volume, M. Jusserand has reiterated his praise of "Jack Wilton" and his belief in Nash as the founder of the British novel of character:—

"In the works of Nash and his imitators, the different parts are badly dovetailed; the novelist is incoherent and incomplete; the fault lies in some degree with the picaresque form itself. Nash, however, pointed out the right road, the road that was to lead to the true novel. He was the first among his compatriots to endeavour to relate in prose a long-sustained story, having for its chief concern: the truth.... No one, Ben Jonson excepted, possessed at that epoch, in so great a degree as himself, a love of the honest truth. With Nash, then, the novel of real life, whose invention in England is generally attributed to Defoe, begins. To connect Defoe with the past of English literature, we must get over the whole of the seventeenth century, and go back to 'Jack Wilton,' the worthy brother of 'Roxana,' 'Moll Flanders,' and 'Colonel Jack.'"

It is to be regretted that Nash made no second adventure in pure fiction. "Jack Wilton," now one of the rarest of his books, was never reprinted in its own age.

How Nash was employed during the next two years, it is not easy to conjecture. When we meet with him once more, the smouldering fire of his quarrel with the Harveys had burst again into flame. "Have with you to Saffron Walden," 1596, is devoted to the chastisement of "the reprobate brace of brothers, to wit, witless Gabriel and ruffling Richard." No fresh public outburst on Harvey's part seems to have led to this attack; but he bragged in private that he had silenced his licentious antagonists. Nash admits that his opponent's last book "has been kept idle by me, in a bye-settle out of sight amongst old shoes and boots almost this two year." Harvey was known to have come from Saffron Walden; Nash invites his readers to accompany him to that town to see what they can discover, and he retails a good deal of lively scandal about the rope-maker's sons. "Have with you" is perhaps the smartest and is certainly the most readable of Nash's controversial volumes. It gives us, too, some interesting fragments of autobiography. Harvey had accused him of "prostituting his pen like a courtisan," and Nash makes this curious and not very lucid statement in selfdefence:—

"Neither will I deny it nor will I grant it. Only thus far I'll go with you, that twice or thrice in a month, when *res est angusta domi*, the bottom of my purse is turned downward, and my conduit of ink will no longer flow for want of reparations, I am fain to let my plough stand still in the midst of a furrow, and follow some of these newfangled Galiardos and Senior Fantasticos, to whose amorous *villanellas* and *quipassas*, I prostitute my pen in hope of gain.... Many a fair day ago have I proclaimed myself to the world Piers Penniless."

Gabriel Harvey must have felt, on reading "Have with you to Saffron Walden," that his antagonist was right in saying that his pen carried "the hot shot of a musket." Unfortunately, while Harvey was smarting under these insulting gibes and jests, the jester himself got into public trouble. Little is known of the circumstance which led the Queen's Privy Council, in the summer of 1597, to throw Nash into the Fleet Prison, but it was connected with the performance of a comedy called "The Isle of Dogs," which gave offence to the authorities. This play was not printed, and is no longer in existence. The Lord Admiral's Company of actors, which produced it, had its licence withdrawn until the 27th of August, when Nash was probably liberated. Gabriel Harvey was not the man to allow this event to go unnoticed. He hurried into print with his "Trimming of Thomas Nash," 1597, a pamphlet of the most outrageous abuse addressed "to the polypragmatical, parasitupocritical and pantophainoudendecontical puppy Thomas Nash," and adorned with a portrait of that gentleman in irons, with heavy gyves upon his ankles. According to Nash, however, the part of "The Isle of Dogs" which was his composition was so trifling in extent that his imprisonment was a gratuitous act of oppression. How the play with this pleasing title offended has not been handed down to us.

Nash was now a literary celebrity, and yet it is at this precise moment that his figure begins to fade out of sight For the next two years he is not known to have made any public appearance. In 1599 he published the best of all his books; it was unfortunately the latest "Nash's Lenten Stuff; or, the Praise of the Red Herring" is an encomium on the hospitable town of Yarmouth, to which, in the autumn of 1597, he had fled for consolation, and in which, through six happy weeks, he had found what he sought The "kind entertainment and benign hospitality" of the compassionate clime of Yarmouth deserve from the poor exile a cordial return, and, accordingly, he sings the praise of the Red Herring as richly as if his mouth were still tingling with the delicate bloater. In this book, Nash is kind enough to explain to us the cause of some of the peculiarities of his style. His endeavour has been to be Italianate, and "of all styles I most affect and strive to imitate Aretine's."

Whether he was deeply read in the works of *il divino Aretino*, we may doubt; but it is easy to see that this Scourge of Princes, the very type of the emancipated Italian of the sixteenth century, might have a vague and dazzling attraction for his little eager English imitator.

Be that as it may, "Lenten Stuff" gives us evidence that Nash had now arrived at a complete mastery of the fantastic and irrelevant manner which he aimed at. This book is admirably composed, if we can bring ourselves to admit that the *genre* is ever admirable. The writer's vocabulary has become opulent, his phrases flash and detonate, each page is full of unconnected sparks and electrical discharges. A sort of aurora borealis of wit streams and rustles across the dusky surface, amusing to the reader, but discontinuous, and insufficient to illuminate the matter in hand. It is extraordinary that a man can make so many picturesque, striking, and apparently apposite remarks, and yet leave us so frequently in doubt as to his meaning. If this was the result of the imitation of Aretino, Nash's choice of a master was scarcely a fortunate one.

Thomas Nash was now thirty-two years of age, and with the publication of "Lenten Stuff" we lose sight of him. His old play of "Summers' Last Will and Testament" was printed in 1600, and he probably died in that year. The song at the close of that comedy or masque reads like the swan-song of its author:—

> Autumn hath all the summer's fruitful treasure; Gone is our sport, fled is poor [Nash's]
> pleasure! Short days, sharp days, long nights come on apace; Ah! who shall hide us from the winter's
> face? Cold doth increase, the sickness will not cease, And here we lie, God knows, with little ease:
> From winter, plague and pestilence, Good Lord, deliver us! London doth mourn, Lambeth is quite
> forlorn, Trades cry, Woe worth that ever they were born; The want of term is town and city's harm.
> Close chambers we do want, to keep us warm; Long banished must we live from our friends: This
> low-built house will bring us to our ends. From winter, plague and pestilence, Good Lord, deliver us!

Whether pestilence or winter slew him, we do not know. In 1601 Fitzgeoffrey published a short Latin elegy on Nash in his "Affaniae," alluding in happy phrase to the twin lightnings of his armed tongue and his terrible pen; and Nash had six lines of tempered praise in "The Return from Parnassus." But all we know of the cause or manner of Nash's death has to be collected from a passage in "A Knight's Conjuring," 1607, written by the satirist on whom his mantle descended, Thomas Dekker. Nash is seen advancing along the Elysian Fields:—

"Marlowe, Greene, and Peele had got under the shades of a large vine, laughing to see Nash, that was but newly come to their college, still haunted with the sharp and satirical spirit that followed him here upon earth; for Nash inveighed bitterly, as he had wont to do, against dry-fisted patrons, accusing them of his untimely death, because if they had given his Muse that cherishment which she most worthily deserved, he had fed to his dying day on fat capons, burnt sack and sugar, and not so desperately have ventured his life and shortened his days by keeping company with pickle herrings."

This looks as though Nash died of a disease attributed to coarse and unwholesome cheap food. His fame proved to be singularly ephemeral. So far as I am aware, no book of his was reprinted after his death, with the single exception of "Christ's Tears over Jerusalem," which was issued again in 1613. His name was mentioned and some interest in his writings was awakened at the close of the next century by Winstanley and by Langbaine, but Oldys, the celebrated antiquary, was the first person who seriously endeavoured to trace the incidents of his life.

Dr. A. B. Grosart saved the works of Nash from all danger of destruction by printing an issue of them, in six volumes, for fifty private subscribers, in 1883-85. But he still remains completely inaccessible to the general reader.

Edmund Gosse.

THE VNFORTVNATE TRAVELLER.
The Life of Iacke Wilton.
LONDON.

To THE RIGHT HONORABLE LORD Henrie Wriothsley,
Earle of sovthhampton, and baron OF TICHFEELD.

Ingenvovs honorable Lord, I know not what blinde custome methodicall antiquity hath thrust vpon vs, to dedicate such books as we publish, to one great man or other; In which respect, least anie man should challenge these my papers as goods vncustomd, and so, extend vpon them as forfeite to contempt, to the seale of your excellent censure loe here I present them to bee seene and allowed. Prize them as high or as low as you list: if you set anie price on them, I hold my labor well satisfide. Long haue I desired to approoue my wit vnto you. My reuerent duetifull thoughts (euen from their infancie) haue been retayners to your glorie. Now at last I haue enforst an opportunitie to plead my deuoted minde. All that in this phantasticall Treatise I can promise, is some reasonable conueyance of historie, & varietie of mirth. By diuers of my good frends haue I been dealt with to employ my dul pen in this kinde, it being a cleane different vaine from other my former courses of writing. How wel or ill I haue done in it, I am ignorant: (the eye that sees roundabout it selfe, sees not into it selfe): only your Honours applauding encouragement hath power to make mee arrogant. Incomprehensible is the heigth of your spirit both in heroical resolution and matters of conceit. Vnrepriueably perisheth that booke whatsoeuer to wast paper, which on the diamond rocke of your iudgement disasterly chanceth to be shipwrackt. A dere louer and cherisher you are, as well of the louers of Poets, as of Poets themselues. Amongst their sacred number I dare not ascribe my selfe, though now and then I speak English: that smal braine I haue, to no further vse I conuert, saue to be kinde to my frends, and fatall to my enemies. A new brain, a new wit, a new stile, a new soule will I get mee, to canonize your name to posteritie, if in this my first attempt I be not taxed of presumption. Of your gracious fauor I despaire not, for I am not altogether Fames outcast. This handfull of leaues I offer to your view, to the leaues on trees I compare, which as they cannot grow of themselues except they haue some branches or boughes to cleaue too, & with whose iuice and sap they be euermore recreated & nourisht: so except these vnpolisht leaues of mine haue some braunch of Nobilitie whereon to depend and cleaue, and with the vigorous nutriment of whose authorized commendation they may be continually fosterd and refresht, neuer wil they grow to the worlds good liking, but forthwith fade and die on the first houre of their birth. Your Lordship is the large spreading branch of renown, from whence these my idle leaues seeke to deriue their whole nourishing: it resteth you either scornfully shake them off, as wormeaten & worthies, or in pity preserue them and cherish them, for some litle summer frute you hope to finde amongst them.

Your Honors in all humble seruice: Tho: Nashe.

TO THE GENTLEMEN READERS,

Gentlemen, in my absence (through the Printers ouersight and my bad writing) in the leaues of C. and D. these errours are ouerslipt:

C. pag. 2. lin. 33. for sweating read sneaking. Pag. 3. li. 1. for hogges read barres, lin. 7. for Calipsus, read Rhæsus. Pag. 4. lin. 34. for Liue read I liue. Pag. 5. li. 14. for vpon his read vpon him his. Pag. 7. lin. 13. for drild read dyu'd. lin. 22. (for colour, read collar nor his hatband).

D. Pag. 1. lin. 2. for blacke read cape. lin. 5. for fastens read thirleth. lin. 7. for badge read budge, lin. 8. for shinne read chinne. lin. 11. for in this begun read thinking in. Pag. 3. lin. 33 for increased then read inclosed them. Pag. 5. lin. 8. for threed button, read brest like a thred bottom. Pag. 8. lin. 3. for Essa read Ossa lin. 4. for dissolution read desolation. lin. 13. betweene also, and but read If you know Christianitie, you know the Fathers of the Church also. lin. 18. for quocunque read qua gente.

Other literall faults there are which I omit

Yours T. N.

[Note.—The foregoing corrigenda are printed as part of the original edition, though they have been corrected in the text.]

THE INDVCTION TO THE DAPPER MOVNSIER PAGES OF THE COVRT.

Gallant squires, haue amongst you: at mumchance I meane not, for so I might chaunce come to short commons, but at *nouus, noua, nouum*, which is in English, newes of the maker. A proper fellow Page of yours called *Iacke Wilton*, by mee commends him vnto you, and hath bequeathed for wast paper heere amongst you certaine pages of his misfortunes. In any case keep them preciously as a *Priuie* token of his good will towards you. If there be some better than other, he craues you would honor them in their death so much, as to drie and kindle *Tobacco* with them: for a need he permits you to wrap veluet pantofles in them also, so they be not woe begone at the heeles, or weather-beaten like a blacke head with graye haires, or mangie at the toes like an ape about the mouth. But as you loue good fellowship and ames ace, rather turne them to stop mustard-pots, than the Grocers shuld haue one patch of them to wrap mace in: a strong hot costly spice it is, which aboue all things hee hates. To anie vse about meate or drinke put them too and spare not, for they cannot doo their Countrey better seruice. Printers are madde whoresons, allow them some of them for napkins. lost a little nerer to the matter and the purpose.*Memorandum*, euerie one of you after the perusing of this Pamphlet, is to prouide him a case of ponyards, that if you come in companie with any man which shall dispraise it or speake against it, you may straight cry Sic respondeo, and giue him the stockado. It stands not with your honors (I assure yee) to haue a Gentleman and a Page abusde in his absence. Secondly, whereas you were wont to sweare men on a pantofle to bee true to your puissaunt order, you shall sweeare them on nothing but this Chronicle of the King of Pages henceforward. Thirdly, it shalbe lawfull for anie whatsoeuer to play with false dice in a corner on the couer of this foresaid Acts and monuments. None of the fraternitie of the minorites shall refuse it for a pawne in the times of famine and necessitie. Euery Stationers stall they passe by whether by day or by night they shall put off their hats too, and make a low leg, in regard their grand printed Capitano is there entoombd. It shalbe flat treason for any of this forementioned catalogue of the point trussers, once to name him within fortie foote of an ale-house. Marry the tauerne is honorable. Many speciall graue articles more had I to giue you in charge, which your wisdomes waiting together at the bottome of the great Chamber staires, or sitting in a porch (your parlament house) may better consider of than I can deliuer: onely let this suffice for a tast to the text & a bit to pull on a good wit with, as a rasher on the coales is to pull on a cup of wine. Heigh passe, come aloft: euery man of you take your places, and heare *Iacke Wilton* tell his owne tale.

THE VNFORTVNATE TRAVELLER.

Abovt that time that the terror of the world, and feauer quartan of the French,*Henrie* the eight, (the onely true subiect of Chronicles) aduanced his standard against the two hundred and fiftie towers of *Turney* and *Turwin*, and had the Empereur and all the nobility of Flanders, Holland, and Brabant as mercenarie attendants on his fulsailed fortune, I *Iacke Wilton* (a Gentleman at lest) was a certaine kinde of an appendix or page, belonging or appertaining in or vnto the confines of the English court, where what my credit was, a number of my creditors that I coosned can testifie, *Cælum petimus stultitia*, which of vs all is not a sinner. Be it knowen to as many as will paie monie inough to peruse my storie, that I followed the campe or the court, or the court & the camp, when *Turwin* lost her maidenhead, & opened her gates to more than *Iane Trosse* did. There did I (soft let me drinke before I goe anie further) raigne sole king of the cans and black iackes, prince of the pigmeis, countie paltaine of cleane strawe and prouant, and to conclude, Lord high regent of rashers of the coles and red herring cobs. *Paulo maiora canamus*: well, to the purpose. What stratagemicall actes and monuments do you thinke an ingenious infant of my age might enact? you will saie, it were sufficient if he slurre a die, pawne his master to the vtmost pennie, & minister the oath on the pantoffle arteficially. These are signes of good education, I must confesse, and arguments of In grace and vertue to proceed. Oh but *Aliquid latet quod non patet*, theres a farther path I must trace: examples confirme, list Lordings to my proceedinges. Whosoeuer is acquainted with the state of a campe, vnderstands that in it be many quarters, & yet not so many as on London bridge. In those quarters are many companies: Much companie, much knauerie, as true as that olde adage, Much curtesie, much subtiltie. Those companies, like a great deale of corne, doe yeeld some chaffe, the corne are cormorants, the chaffe are good fellowes, which are quickly blowen to nothing, with bearing a light hart in a light purse. Amongst this chaffe was I winnowing my wits to liue merily, and by my troth so I did: the prince could but command men spend theyr bloud in his seruice, I coulde make them spend all the monie they had for my pleasure. But pouerty in the end parts frends, though I was prince of their purses, and exacted of my vnthrift subiects, as much liquid allégeance as anie keisar in the world could do, yet where it is not to be had the king must loose his right, want cannot be withstood, men can doe no more than they can doe, what remained then, but the foxes case must help, when the lions skin is out at the elbowes.

There was a Lord in the campe, let him be a Lord of misrule, if you wil, for he kept a plaine alehouse without welt or gard of anie Iuibush, and solde syder and cheese by pint and by pound to all that came (at that verie name of syder, I can but sigh, there is so much of it in renish wine now a dayes). Wei, *Tendit ad sydera virtus*, thers great vertue belongs (I can tell you) to a cup of syder, and verie good men haue solde it, and at sea it is *Aqua cœlestis*, but thats neither heere nor there, if it had no other patrone but this peere of quart pots to authorize it, it were sufficient This great Lorde, this worthie Lord, this noble Lord, thought no scorne (Lord haue mercy vpon vs) to haue his great veluet breeches larded with the droppings of this daintie liquor, & yet he was an olde senator, a cauelier of an ancient house, as it might appeare by the armes of his ancestrie, drawen very amiably in chalke, on the in side of his tent doore.

He and no other was the man, I chose out to damne with a lewd monylesse deuice: for comming to him on a daie, as he was counting his barrels, & setting the price in chalke on the head of euerie one of them, I did my dutie verie deuoutly, and tolde his*alie* honor, I had matters of some secrecie to impart vnto him, if it pleased him to grant me priuate audience. With me young *Wilton* quoth he, marie and shalt: bring vs a pint of syder of a fresh tap into the three cups here, wash the pot, so into a backe roome he lead mee, where after hee had spit on his finger, and pickt off two or three moats of his olde moth eaten veluet cap, and spunged and wrong all the rumatike driuell from his ill fauoured Goates beard, he badde me declare my minde, and there vpon he dranke to me on the same. I vp with a long circumstance, alias, a cunning shift of the seuenteenes, & discourst vnto him what entire affection I had borne him time out of mind, partly for the high discent and linage from whence he sprung, & partly for the tender care and prouident respect he had of poore soldiers, that whereas the vastitie of that place (which afforded them no indifferent supplie of drinke or of victuals) might humble them to some extremity, and so weaken their hands, he vouchsafed in his own person to be a victualer to the campe (a rare example of magnificence & honorable curtesie) and diligently prouided, that without farre trauel, euery man might for his money haue syder and cheese his bellyfull, nor did he sell his cheese by the way onely, or his syder by the great, but abast himselfe with his owne hands, to take a shoomakers knife (a homely instrument for such a high personage to touch) and cut it out equally like a true iusticiarie, in little pennyworthes, that it woulde doo a man good for to looke vpon. So likewise of his syder, the pore man might haue his moderate draught of it (as there is a moderation in all things) as well for his doit or his dandiprat, as the rich man for his halfe souse or his denier. Not so much, quoth I, but this tapsters linnen apron, which you weare before you, to protect your appareil from the imperfections of the spigot, most amply bewrais your lowly minde. I speake it with teares, too fewe such humble spirited noble men haue we, that will draw drinke in linen aprons. Why you are euerie childs felow, any man that comes vnder the name of a souldier and a goodfellowe, you will sitte and beare companie to the last pot, yea, and you take in as good part the homely phrase of mine host heeres to you, as if one saluted you by all the titles of your baronie. These considerations, I saie, which the world suffers to slippe by in the channell of carelesnes, haue moued me in ardent zeale of your welfare, to forewarne you of some dangers that haue beset you & your barrels. At the name of dangers hee start up, and bounst with his fist on the boord so hard, that his Tapster ouerhearing him, cried anone anone sir, by and by, and came and made a low leg and askt him what he lackt. Hee was readie to haue striken his Tapster, for interrupting him in attention of this his so much desired relation, but for feare of displeasing me he moderated his furie, and onely sending him for the other fresh pint, wild him looke to the barre, and come when hee is cald with a deuilles name. Well, at his earnest importunitie, after I had moistned my lips, to make my lie runne glib to his iourneies end, forward I went as followeth. It chaunced me the other night, amongst other pages, to attend where the king with his Lords, and many chiefe leaders sate in counsel, there amongst sundrie serious matters that were debated, and intelligences from the enemy giuen vp, it was priuily informed (no villains to these priuie informers) that you, euen you that I now speak to, would I had no tongue to tell the rest, by this drink it grieues me so I am not able to repeate it. Nowe was my dronken Lord redie to hang himself for the end of the ful point, and ouer my necke he throws himselfe verie lubberly, and intreated me as I was a proper young Gentleman, and euer lookt for pleasure at his hands, soone to rid him out of this hell of suspence, & resolue him of the rest, then fell hee on his knees, wrong his handes, and I thinke, on my conscience, wept out all the syder that he had dronke in a weeke before, to moue me to haue pitie on him, he rose and put his rustie ring on my finger, gaue me his greasie purse with that single money that was in it, promised to make mee his heire, & a thousand more fauours, if I would expire the miserie of his vnspeakable tormenting vncertaintie. I being by nature inclined to *Mercie* (for indeed I knew two or three good wenches of that name) bad him harden his eares, & not make his eyes abortiue before their time, and he should haue the inside of my brest turnd outward, heare such a tale as would tempt the vtmost strength of life to attend it, and not die in the middest of it. Why (quoth I) my selfe, that am but a poore childish welwiller of yours, with the verie thought, that a man of your desert and state, by a number of pesants and varlets should be so iniuriously abused in hugger mugger, haue wept al my vrine vpward. The wheele vnder our Citie bridge, carries not so much water ouer the city, as my braine hath welled forth gushing streames of sorow. I haue wept so immoderatly and lauishly, that I thought verily my palat had bin turned to pissing conduit in London. My eies haue bin dronk, outragiously dronke, with giuing but ordinary entercourse through their sea-circled Ilands to my distilling dreariment What shal I saie? that which malice hath sayde is the meere ouerthrow & murder of your daies. Change not your colour, none can slander a cleere conscience to it selfe, receiue all your fraught of misfortune in at once.

It is buzzed in the kings head that you are a secret friend to the enemy, & vnder pretence of getting a license to furnish the campe with syder and such like prouant, you haue furnisht the enemy, and in emptie barrells sent letters of discouerie, and come innumerable, I might well haue left here, for by this time his white liuer had mixt it selfe with the white of his eie, & both were turned vpwardes, as if they had offered themselues a fayre white for death to shoote at. The troth was, I was verie loth mine hoste and I should parte to heauen with dry lips, wherefore the best meanes that I could imagine to wake him out of his traunce, was to crie loude in his eare, hough host, whats to pay, will no man looke to the reckning heere and in plaine veritie, it tooke expected effect, for with the noise he started and bustled, like a man that had beene scard with fyre out of his sleepe, and ranne hastily to his Tapster, and all to belaboured him about the eares, for letting Gentlemen call so long and not looke in to them. Presently he remembred himselfe, and had like to haue fallen into his memento againe, But that I met him halfe waies, and askt his Lordship what he meant to slip his necke out of the coller so sodainly, and being reuiued, strike his tapster so rashly.

Oh, quoth he, I am bought & solde for doing my Country such good seruice as I haue done. They are afraid of mee, because my good deedes haue brought me into such estimation with the communalty, I see, I see it is not for the lambe to liue with the wolfe.

The world is well amended, thought I, with your Sidership, such another fortie yeeres nappe together as *Epemenides* had, would make you a perfect wise man. Answere me, quoth he, my wise young *Wilton*, is it true that I am thus vnderhand dead and buried by these bad tongues?

Nay, quoth I, you shall pardon me, for I haue spoken too much alreadie, no definitiue sentence of death shall march out of my wel meaning lips, they haue but lately suckt milke, and shall they so sodainly change theyr food and seeke after bloud?

Oh but, quoth he, a mans friend is his friend, fill the other pint Tapster, what sayd the king, did hee beleeue it when hee heard it, I pray thee say, I sweare to thee by my nobility, none in the worlde shall euer be made priuie, that I receiued anie light of this matter from thee.

That firme affiance, quoth I, had I in you before, or else I would neuer haue gone so farre ouer the shooes, to plucke you out of the mire. Not to make many wordes (since you will needs know) the king saies flatly, you are a miser & a snudge, and he neuer hopt better of you. Nay then (quoth he) questionlesse some planet that loues not syder hath conspired against me. Moreouer, which is worse, the king hath vowed to giue *Turwin* one hot breakfast, onely with the bungs that hee will plucke out of your barrells. I cannot staie at this time to reporte each circumstance that passed, but the only counsell that my long cherished kinde inclination can possibly contriue, is now in your olde daies to be liberall, such victuals or prouisions as you haue, presently distribute it frankly amongst poore souldiers, I would let them burst their bellies with syder, and bathe in it, before I would runne into my Princes ill opinion for a whole sea of it. The hunter pursuing the beauer for his stones, hee bites them off, and leaues them behinde for him to gather vp, whereby he liues quiet. If greedie hunters and hungry teltales pursue you, it is for a little pelfe which you haue, cast it behind you, neglect it, let them haue it, lest it breed a further inconuenience. Credit my aduice, you shall finde it propheticall, and thus I haue discharged the parte of a poore friend. With some few like phrases of ceremonie, your honors suppliant, & so forth, and farewel my good youth, I thanke thee and will remember thee, we parted. But the next daie I thinke we had a dole of syder, syder in boules, in scuppets, in helmets, & to conclude, if a man would haue fild his bootes full, there hee might haue had it, prouant thrust it selfe into poore souldiers pockets whether they would or no. We made fiue peals of shot into the towne together, of nothing but spiggots and faussets of discarded emptie barrels: euerie vnderfoote soildiour had a distenanted tunne, as *Diogenes* had his tub to sleepe in, I my selfe got as many confiscated Tapsters aprons, as made me a Tent, as bigge as any ordinarie commanders in the field. But in conclusion, my welbeloued Baron of double beere got him humbly on his marybones to the king, and complained hee was olde and striken in yeres, and had nere an heire to cast at a dogge, wherefore if it might please his maiesty to take his lands into his hands, and allowe him some reasonable pension to liue on, hee shoulde bee meruailous wel pleased: as for the warres, he was wearie of them, and yet as long as highnes shoulde venture his owne person, hee would not flinch a foot, but make his withered bodie a buckler, to beare off anie blow that should be aduanced agaynst him.

The king meruailing at this strange alteration of his great marchant of syder (for so hee woulde often pleasantly tearme him), with a little further talke bolted out the whole complotment Then was I pittifully whipt for my holy day lie, although they made themselues merrie with it many a faire winters euening after.

Yet notwithstanding his good asseheaded honor mine host, perseuered in his former simple request to the king to accept of the surrender of his landes, and allowe him a beadsmanry or out-brother-ship of brachet, which at length, through his vehement instancie tooke effect, and the king ieastingly sayd, since he would needs haue it so, he would distrain on part of his land for impost of syder, which hee was behinde hande with him, and neuer payd.

This was one of my famous atchieuements, insomuch as I neuer light vpon the like famous foole, but I haue done a thousand better ieasts if they had bin bookt in order as they were begotten. It is pittie posteritie shoulde bee depriued of such precious recordes, and yet there is no remedie, and yet there is to, for when all fayles, welfare a good memorie. Gentle readers (looke you be gentle now since I haue cald you so) as freely as my knauerie was mine owne, it shall be yours to vse in the way of honestie.

Euen in this expedition of Turwin (for the king stoode not long thrumming of buttons there) it happened me fall out (I would it had fallen out otherwise for his sake) with an vgly mechanical Captaine. You must thinke in an armie, where tronchios are in their state house, it is a flat stab once to name a Captaine without cappe in hand. Well, suppose hee was a Captaine, & had nere a good cap of his owne, but I was faine to lend him one of my Lords cast veluet caps, and a weatherbeaten feather, wherewith he threatned his souldiers a farre off, as Iupiter is sayde, with the shaking of his haire to make heauen and earth to quake: suppose out of the paringes of a paire of false dice, I apparelled both him and my selfe many a time and oft: and surely not to slander the deuill, if anie man euer deserued the golden dice, the king of the Parthians sent to *Demetrius* it was I, I had the right vaine of sucking vp a die twixt the dintes of my fingers, not a creuise in my hande but coulde swallowe a quater trey for a neede: in the line of life many a dead lifte dyd there lurke, but it was nothing towards the maintenance of a family. This Monsieur Capitano eate vp the creame of my earnings, and *Crede mihi res est ingeniosa dare*, any man is a fine fellow as long as he hath anie monie in his purse. That monie is like the marigolde, which opens and shuts with the Sunne, if fortune smileth, or one be in fauour, it floweth: if the euening of age comes on, or he falleth into disgrace, it fadeth and is not to be found. I was my crafts master though I was but yong, and could as soone decline *Nominatiuo hic asinus*, as a greater clarke, wherefore I thought it not conuenient my soldado should haue my purse anie longer for his drumme to play vppon, but I woulde giue him Iacke drummes entertainment, and send him packing. This was my plot, I knewe a peece of seruice of intelligence, which was presently to bee done, that required a man with all his fiue senses to effect it, and would ouefthrow anie foole that should vndertake it, to this seruice did I animate and egge my foresayd costes and charges, alias, senior veluet-cappe, whose head was not encombered with too much forecast, and comming to him in his cabbin about dinner time, where I found him verie deuoutly paring of his nailes for want of other repast, I entertained him with this solemne oration.

Captaine, you perceiue how neere both of vs are driuen, the dice of late are growen as melancholy as a dog, high men and low men both prosper alike, langrets, fullams, and all the whole fellowshippe of them will not affoord a man his dinner, some other means must be inuented to preuent imminent extremitie. My state, you are not ignorant, depends on trencher seruice, your aduancement must be deriued from the valour of your arme. In the delayes of siege, desert hardly gets a daye of hearing, tis gowns must direct and guns enact all the wars that is to bee made against walls. Resteth no waie for you to climbe sodainly, but by doing some straunge stratageme, that the like hath not bene heard of heeretofore, and fitly at this instant occasion is ministred.

There is a feate the king is desirous to haue wrought on some great man of the enemies side, marie it requireth not so much resolution as discretion to bring it to passe, and yet resolution inough shalbe showen in it to, being so full of hazardous ieopardy as it is, harke in your eare, thus it is. Without more drumbling or pausing, if you will vndertake it, and worke it through stitch (as you may ere the king hath determined which waie to goe about it) I warrant you are made while you liue, you neede not care which waie your staffe falles, if it proue not so, then cut off my head.

Oh my auditors, had you seene him how he stretcht out his lims, scratcht his scabd elbowes at this speech, how hee set his cap ouer his eie browes like a polititian, and then folded his armes one in another, & nodded with the head, as who should saie, let the French beware, for they shall finde me a deuill, if I say, you had seen but halfe the actions that he vsed of shrucking vp his shoulders, smiling scornfully, playing with his fingers on his buttons, and biting the lip, you wold haue laught your face and your knees together. The yron being hot, I thought to lay on loade, for in anie case I would not haue his humour coole. As before I layd open vnto him the briefe summe of the seruice, so now I began to vrge the honorablenesse of it, and what a rare thing it was to be a right politician, how much esteemd of kings and princes, and how diuerse of meane parentage haue come to be monarches by it. Then I discourst of the qualities and properties of him in euerie respect, how lyke the wolfe he must drawe the breath from a man before he be seen, how lyke a hare he must sleepe with his eyes open, how as the Eagle in flying casts dust in the eyes of crowes & other foules, for to blind them, so he must cast dust in the eies of his enimies, delude their sight by one meanes or other, y they diue not into his subtilties: how he must be familiar with all & trust none, drinke, carouse and lecher with him out of whom he hopes to wring anie matter, sweare and forsweare, rather than be suspected, and in a word, haue the art of dissembling at his fingers ends as perfect as anie courtier.

Perhaps (quoth I) you may haue some few greasie cauelliers that will seeke to disswade you from it, and they will not sticke to stand on theyr three halfe pennie honour, swearing and staring that a man were better be an hangman than an intelligencer, and call him a sneaking eausdropper, a scraping hedgecreeper, and a piperly pickthanke, but you must not bee discouraged by theyr talke, for the most part of those beggerly contemners of wit, are huge burlybond butchers like *Aiax*, good for nothing but to strike right downe blowes on a wedge with a cleauing beetle, or stande hammering all daie vppon barres of yron. The whelpes of a Beare neuer grow but sleeping, and these bearewards hauing big limmes shall bee preferd though they doe nothing. You haue read stories, (He bee sworne he neuer lookte in booke in his life) how many of the Romane worthies were there that haue gone as spies into theyr enemies campe? *Vlysses, Nestor, Diomed*, went as spies together in the night into the tentes of *Rhosus* and intercepted *Dolon* the spie of the Troians: neuer anie discredited the trade of intelligencers but *Iudas*, & he hanged himselfe. Danger will put wit into anie man. *Architas* made a wooden doue to flie: by which proportion I see no reason that the veryest blocke in the world should despayre of anie thing. Though nature be contrarie inclined, it may be altered, yet vsually those whome she denies her ordinarie giftes in one thing, she doubles them in another. That which the asse wants in wit, hee hath in honestie, who euer sawe him kicke or winch, or vse anie iades trickes, though he liue an hundred yeeres you shall never heare that he breakes pasture. Amongst men, hee that hath not a good wit, lightly hath a good yron memorie, and he that hath neither of both, hath some bones to carrie burthens. Blinde men haue better noses than other men: the buls horns serue him as well as hands to fight withall: the lions pawes are as good to him as a polaxe, to knock downe anie that resists him: so the Bores tushes serue him in better stead than a sword and buckler, what need the snaile care for eyes, when he feeles the waie with his two homes, as well as if hee were as sharpe sighted as a decypherer. There is a fish that hauing no wings, supportes her selfe in the ayre with her finnes. Admit that you had neither wit nor capacitie, as sure in my iudgement there is none equall vnto you in idiotisme, yet if you haue simplicitie and secrecie, serpents themselues will thinke you a serpent, for what serpent is there but hydeth his sting: and yet whatsoeuer bee wanting, a good plausible alluring tong in such a man of imployment can hardly be spard, which as the forenamed serpent, with his winding tayle fetcheth in those that come neere him: so with a rauishing tale, it gathers all mens heartes vnto him, which if hee haue not, let him neuer looke to ingender by the mouth, as rauens and doues doe, that is, mount or be great by vndermining. Sir, I am assertayned that all these imperfections I speake off, in you haue theyr naturall resiance, I see in your face, that you were borne with the swallow, to feede flying, to get much treasure and honour by trauell. None so fit as you for so important an enterprise, our vulgar reputed polititians are but flyes swimming on the streame of subtiltie superficially in comparison of your singularitie, theyr blind narrowe eyes cannot pearce into the profunditie of hypocrisie, you alone with *Palamed*, can pry into *Vlysses* madde counterfeting, you can discerne *Achilles* from a chamber maide, though he be deckt with his spindle and distaffe: as *Ioue* dining with *Licaon* could not be beguiled with humane flesh drest like meate, so no humane braine may goe beyond you, none beguile you, you gull all, all feare you, loue you, stoupe to you. Therefore, good sir, be rulde by mee, stoupe your fortune so lowe, as to bequeath your selfe wholy to this businesse.

This siluer sounding tale made such sugred harmonie in his eares, that with the sweete meditation, what a more than myraculous polititian he should be, and what kingly promotion should come tumbling on him thereby, he could haue found in his heart to haue packt vp his pipes & to haue gone to heauen without a baite, yea, hee was more inflamed and rauishte with it than a young man called *Tauritnontanus* was with the Phrigian melodie, who was so incensed and fyred therewith, that he would needes runne presently vpon it, and set a curtizans house on fire that had angered him.

No remedie there was but I must helpe to furnish him with monie, I did so, as who wil not make his enemy a bridge of golde to flie by. Verie earnestly he coniurd me to make no man liuing priuie to his departure in regard of his place and charge, and on his honour assured mee his returne shoulde bee verie short and succesfull, I, I, shorter by the necke, thought I, in the meane time let this be thy posie, *I liue in hope to scape the rope.*

Gone he is, God send him good shipping to Wapping, & by this time, if you will, let him bee a pittifull poore fellowe, and vndone for euer, for mine owne part, if he had bin mine owne brother, I coulde haue done no more for him than I did, for straight after his backe was turnd, I went in all loue & kindnesse to the Marshall generall of the field, & certefide him that such a man was lately fled to the enemie, and gotte his place beggd for another immediatly. What became of him after you shall heare. To the enemie he went and offered his seruice, ratling egregiously on the king of England, he swore, as he was a Gentleman and a souldier, hee would bee reuenged on him, and let but the king of France follow his counsell, hee woulde driue him from *Turwin* wals yet ere ten dayes to an end. All these were good humours, but the tragedie followeth. The French king hearing of such a prating fellow that was come, was desirous to see him, but yet he feared treason, wherfore he wild one of his minions to take vpon him his person, and he would stand by as a priuate man whilest hee was examined. Why should I vse anie idle delayes? In was Captaine Gogges wounds brought, after he was throughly searched, not a louse in his doublet was let passe, but was askt *Queuela*, and chargd to stand in the kings name, the mouldes of his buttons they turnd out, to see if they were not bullettes couered ouer with thread, the codpeece in his deuills breeches (for they were then in fashion) they sayd playnly was a case for a pistoll, if hee had had euer a hobnaile in his shooes it had hangde him, & he shuld neuer haue knowen who had harmd him, but as lucke was, he had not a mite of anie mettal about him, he tooke part with none of the foure ages, neither the golden age, the siluer age, the brasen nor the yron age, onely his purse was aged in emptinesse, and I thinke verily a puritane, for it kept it selfe from any pollution of crosses. Standing before the supposed king, he was askt what he was, and wherefore he came. To the which in a glorious bragging humour he aunswered, that hee was a gentleman, a captaine commander, a chiefe leacjer, that came away from the king of England vppon discontentment. Questiond particular of the cause of his discontentment, hee had not a word to blesse himself with, yet faine he would haue patcht out a poltfoote tale, but (God he knowes) it had not one true legge to stand on. Then began he to smell on the villaine so rammishly, that none there but was readie to rent him in peeces, yet the minion king kept in his cholar, and propounded vnto him farther, what of the king of Englands secrets (so aduantageable) he was priuie to, as might remoue him from the siege of Turwin in three daies. Hee sayde diuerse, diuerse matters, which askt longer conference, but in good honestie they were lies, which he had not yet stampt. Heereat the true king stept forth, and commanded to lay handes on the lozell, and that he should be tortured to confesse the truth, for he was a spie and nothing else.

He no sooner sawe the wheele and the torments set before him, but he cride out like a rascall, and sayde hee was a poore Captaine in the English camp, suborned by one *Iacke Wilton* (a noble mans page) and no other, to come and kill the French king in a brauery and returne, and that he had no other intention in the world.

This confession could not choose but moue them all to laughter, in that he made it as light a matter to kill their king and come backe, as to goe to Islington and eate a messe of creame, and come home againe, nay, and besides hee protested that he had no other intention, as if that were not inough to hang him.

Adam neuer fell till God made fooles, all this coulde not keepe his ioyntes from ransacking on the wheele, for they vowed either to make him a confessor or a martir in a trice, when still he sung all one song, they tolde the king he was a foole, and some shrewd head had knauishly wrought on him, wherefore it should stand with his honour to whip him out of the campe and send him home. That perswasion tooke place, and soundly was he lasht out of theyr liberties, and sent home by a Heralde with this message, that so the king his master hoped to whip home all the English fooles verie shortly: answere was returned, that that shortlie, was a long lie, and they were shrewde fooles that shoulde driue the French man out of his kingdome, and make him glad with Corinthian *Dionisius* to play the schoole-master.

The Herald being dismist, our afflicted intelligencer was cald *coram nobis*, how he spedde, iudge you, but something hee was adiudged to. The sparowe for his lecherie liueth but a yeere, he for his trecherie was turnd on the toe, *Plura dolor prohibet.*

Here let me triumph a while, and ruminate a line or two on the excellence of my wit, but I will not breath neither til I haue disfraughted all my knauerie.

Another Swizer Captaine that was farre gone for want of the wench, I led astraie most notoriously, for he beeing a monstrous vnthrift of battle axes (as one that cared not in his anger to bid flie out scuttels to fiue score of them) and a notable emboweller of quart pots, I came disguised vnto him in the forme of a halfe a crowne wench, my gowne and attire according to the custome the in request. I wis I had my curtesies in cue or in quart pot rather, for they dyu'd into the very entrailes of the dust, and I simpered with my countenance lyke a porredge pot on the fire when it first begins to seeth. The sobrietie of the circumstance is, that after he had courted me and all, and giuen me the earnest pennie of impietie, some sixe crownes at the least for an antipast to iniquitie, I fained an impregnable excuse to be gone, and neuer came at him after. Yet left I not here, but committed a little more scutcherie. A companie of coystrell clarkes (who were in band with sathan, and not of anie souldiers collar nor his hatband) pincht a number of good mindes to Godward of theyr prouant. They would not let a dram of dead pay ouerslip them, they would not lend a groat of the weeke to come, to him that had spent his money before this weeke was done. They outfaced the greatest and most magnanimious servitours in their sincere and finigraphicall cleane shirts and cuffes. A lowse that was anie Gentlemans companion they thought scorne of, their nere bitten beardes must in a deuils name bedewdeuerie daiewith rosewater, hogges could haue nere a hayre on theyr backes, for making them rubbing brushes to rouse theyr crab lice. They woulde in no wise permitte that the moates in the Sunnebeames should be full mouthde beholders of theyr cleane phinikde appareil, theyr shooes shined as bright as a slike-stone, theyr handes troubled and soyled more water with washing, than the camell doth, that nere drinkes till the whole streame bee troubled. Summarily, neuer anie were so fantastical the one halfe as they. My masters you may conceiue of me what you list, but I thinke confidently I was ordayned Gods scourge from aboue for theyr daintie finicalitie. The houre of theyr punishment could no longer be proroged, but vengeance must haue at them at al a ventures. So it was, that the most of these aboue named goosequil braccahadocheos were meere cowards and crauens, and durst not so much as throw a penfull of inke into the enimies face, if proofe were made, wherefore on the experience of their pusellanimitie I thought to raise the foundation of my roguerie. What did I now but one daie made a false alarum in the quarter where they laie, to trie how they would stand to theyr tackling, and with a pittifull outcrie warned them to flie, for there was treason afoot, they were inuironed and beset. Upon the first watch worde of treason that was giuen, I thinke they betooke them to theyr heeles verie stoutly, left theyr penne and inke-hornes and papers behinde them for spoile, resigned theyr deskes, with the mony that was in them to the mercie of the vanquisher, and in fine, left mee & my fellowes (their foole-catchers) Lords of the field: how wee dealt with them, their disburdened deskes canne best tell, but this I am assured, we fared the better for it a fortnight of fasting dayes after. I must not place a volume in the precincts of a pamphlet, sleepe an houre or two, and dreame that Turney and Turwin is wonne, that the king is shipt againe into England, and that I am close at harde meate at Windsore or at Hampton court. What will you in your indifferent opinions allow me for my trauell, no more seigniorie ouer the Pages than I had before? yes, whether you will parte with so much probable friendly suppose or no, He haue it in spite of your heartes. For your instruction and godly consolation, bee informed, that at that time I was no common squire, no vndertroden

16

torch-bearer, I had my feather in my cap as big as a flag in the foretop, my French doublet gelte in the belly as though (lyke a pig readie to be spitted) all my guts had beene pluckt out, a paire of side paned hose that hung down like two scales filled with Holland cheeses, 'my long stock that sate close to my docke, and smoothered not a scab or a leacherous hairie sinew on the calfe of my legge, my rapier pendant like a round sticke fastned in the tacklings for skippers the better to climbe by, my cape cloake of blacke cloth, ouerspreading my backe lyke a thornbacke, or an Elephantes eare, that hanges on his shoulders lyke a countrie huswiues banskin, which shee thirleth her spindle on, and in consummation of my curiositie, my handes without gloues, all a more French, and a blacke budge edging of a beard on the vpper lip, & the like sable auglet of excrements in the first rising of the anckle of my chinne. I was the first that brought in the order of passing into the court which I deriued from the common word *Qui passa*, and the heralds phrase of armes Passant, thinking in sincerie, hee was not a Gentleman, nor his armes currant, who was not first past by the pages. If anie prentise or other came into the court that was not a Gentleman, I thought it was an indignitie to the preheminence of the court to include such a one, and could not be salud except we gaue him armes Passant, to make him a Gentleman. Besides, in Spaine, none compasse anie farre waie but he must be examined what he is, & giue three pence for his passe. In which regard it was considered of by the common table of the cupbearers, what a perilsome thing it was to let anie stranger or outdweller approch so neere the precincts of the Prince, as the great chamber, without examining what he was and giuing him his passe, whereuppon we established the lyke order, but tooke no monie of them as they did, onelie for a signe that he had not past our hands vnexamined, wee set a red marke on either of his eares, and so let him walke as authenticall. I must not discouer what vngodly dealing we had with the blacke iackes, or how oft I was crowned king of the dronkards with a court cuppe, let mee quietly descend to the waining of my youthfull dayes, and tell a little of the sweating sicknesse, that made me in a cold sweate take my heeles and runne out of England.

This sweating sicknesse, was a disease that a man then might catch and neuer goe to a hothouse. Many masters desire to haue such semants as would worke till they sweate againe, but in those dayes he that sweat neuer wrought againe. That Scripture then was not thought so necessarie, which sayes, Earne thy liuing with the sweat of thy browes, for then they earnd their dying with the sweat of their browes. It was inough if a fat man did but trusse his points, to turne him ouer the pearch: mother*Cornelius* tub why it was lyke hell, he that came into it neuer came out of it Cookes that stande continually basting theirfaces before the fire, were nowe all cashierd with this sweat into kitchinstuffe: theyr hall fell in to the kings handes for want of one of the trade to vpholde it. Feltmakers and furriers, what the one with the hot steame of their wooll new taken out of the pan, and the other with the contagious heate of their slaughter budge and connyskins, died more thicke than of the pestilence: I haue seene an olde woman at that season hauing three chins, wipe them all away one after another, as they melted to water, and left her selfe nothing of a mouth but an vpper chap. Looke how in May or the heat of Summer we lay butter in water for feare it shuld melte awaie, so then were men faine to wet their clothes in water as Diers doo, and hide themselues in welles from the heate of the Sunne.

Then happie was he that was an asse, for nothing wyll kill an asse but colde, and none dide but with extreame heate. The fishes called Seastarres, that burne one another by excessiue heate, were not so contagious as one man that had the sweate was to another. Masons paid nothing for haire to mix their lime, nor giouers to stuffe their balls with, for then they had it for nothing, it dropt off mens heads and beardes faster than anie Barber could shaue it. O if haire breeches had then beene in fashion, what a fine world had it beene for Taylers, and so it was a fine world for Tailers neuerthelesse, for hee that could make a garment sleightest and thinnest, carried it awaie. Cutters I can tell you, then stood vpon it, to haue their trade one of the twelue Companies, for who was it then that would not haue his doublet cut to the skin, and his shirt cut into it to, to make it more colde. It was as much as a mans life was worth, once to name a freeze ierken, it was treason for a fat grosse man to come within fiue miles of the court, I heard where they dide vp all in one family, and not a mothers childe escapt, insomuch as they had but an Irish rug lockt vp in a presse, and not laide vpon anie bedde neither, if those that were sicke of this maladie slept on it, they neuer wakt more. Phisitions with their simples, in this case were simple fellowes, and knew not which way to bestir them. Galen might goe shop the gander for anie good he could doe, his secretatyes had so long called him diuine, that now he had lost all his vertue vpon earth. *Hippocrates* might well helpe Almanack makers, but here he had not a worde to saie, a man might sooner catch the sweate with plodding ouer him to no end, than cure the sweat with any of his impotent principles. *Paracelsus* with his spirit of the butterie, and his spirits of minerals, could not so much as say, God amend him, to the matter. *Plus erat in artifice quant arte*, there was more infection in the phisition himselfe than his arte could cure. This mortalitie first began amongst olde men, for they taking a pride to haue their breasts loose basted with tedious beards, kept their houses so hot with these hairy excrements, that not so much but their very wals sweat out salt Peter, with the smoothering perplexitie, nay a number of them had meruailous hot breaths, which sticking in the briers of their bushie beardes, could not choose, but (as close aire long imprisoned) engender corruption. Wiser was our brother *Bankes* of these latter dais, who made his iugling horse a cut, for feare if at anie time hee should foist, the stinke sticking in his thicke bushie taile might be noisome to his auditors. Should I tell you how many purseuants with red noses, and sargeants with precious faces shrunke away in this sweat, you would not beleeue me. Euen as the Salamander with his very sight blasteth apples on the trees, so a purseuant or a sargeant at this present, with the verie reflexe of his fine facias, was able to spoile a man a farre of. In some places of the world there is no shadow of the sunne, *Diebus illis* if it had bene so in England, the generation of *Brute* had died all and some. To knit vp this description in a pursuat, so feruent and scorching was the burning aire which inclosed them, that the most blessed man then aliue, would haue thoght that God had done fairely by him, if he had turnde him to a goat, for goates take breath not at the mouth or nose only, but at y eares also.

Take breath how they would, I vowd to tarrie no longer amongst them. As at Turwin I was a demie souldier in iest, so now I became a martiallist in earnest. Ouer sea with my implements I got me, where hearing the king of France and the Swizers were together by the ears, I made towards them as fast as I could, thinking to thrust my selfe into that faction that was strongest It was my good lucke or my ill, I know not which, to come iust to ye fighting of the battel, where I sawe a wonderfull spectacle of bloud shed on both sides, here the vnwildie swizers wallowing in their gore, like an oxe in his doung, there the sprightly French sprawling and turning on the stayned grasse, like a roach newe taken out of the streame, all the ground was strewed as thicke with battle axes, as the carpenters yard with chips. The plaine appeared like a quagmire, ouerspread as it was with trampled dead bodies. In one place might you beholde a heape of dead murthered men ouerwhelmed with a falling steed, in stead of a tombe stone, in another place a bundle of bodies fettered together in theyr owne bowels, and as the tyrant Romane Empereurs vsed to tie condemned liuing caitifes face to face to dead corses, so were the halfe liuing here mixt with squeazed carcases long putrifide. Anie man might giue armes that was an actor in that battell, for there were more armes and legs scattered in the field that daie, than will be gathered vp till dooms daie, the French king himselfe in this conflict was much distressed, the braines of his owne men sprinkled in his face, thrice was his courser slaine vnder him, and thrice was hee strucke on the breast with a speare, but in the end, by the helpe of the Venetians, the Heluesians or Swizers were subdude, and he crowned victor, a peace concluded, and the cittie of Millain surrendered vnto him, as a pledge of reconciliation. That warre thus blowen ouer, and the seueral bands dissolued, like a crow that still followes aloofe where there is carrion, I flew me ouer to Munster in Germanie, which an Anabaptisticall brother named *Iohn Leiden* kepte at that instant against the Emperor and the Duke of Saxonie. Here I was in good hope to set vp my staffe for some reasonable time, deeming that no Citie would driue it to a siege except they were able to holde out, and pretily well had these Munsterians held out, for they kept the Emperour and the Duke of Saxonie sound plaie for the space of a yeere, and longer wold haue done, but that dame famine came amongst them, wherevppon they were forst by messengers to agree vpon a daie of fight, when according to theyr anabaptisticall errour they might be all new christned in theyr owne bloud.

That daie come, flourishing entered *Iohn Leiden* the botcher into the field, with a scarfe made of lists, like a bowcase, a crosse on his brest like a thred bottom, a round twilted Tailers cushion buckled lyke a tancard bearers deuice to his shoulders for a target, the pike whereof was a packe needle, a tough prentises club for his speare, a great brewers cow on his back for a corslet, and on his head for a helmet a huge high shoo with the bottome turnd vpward, embossed as full of hobnailes as euer it might sticke, his men were all base handie craftes, as coblers, and curriers, and tinkers, whereof some had barres of yron, some hatchets, some coole staues, some dung forks, some spades, some mattockes, some wood kniues, some addsses for theyr weapons, he that was best prouided, had but a peece of a rustie browne bill brauely fringed with cobwebbes to fight for him: perchance here and there you might see a felow that had a canker eaten seul on his head, which serued him and his ancestors for a chamber pot two hundred yeeres, and another that had bent a couple of yron dripping pans armourwise, to fence his backe and his belly, another that had thrust a payre of dry olde bootes as a breast plate before his belly of his doublet, because he would not be dangerously hurt: another that had twilted all his trusse full of counters, thinking if the enemie shoulde take him, he would mistake them for golde, and so saue his life for his money. Very deuout asses they were, for all they were so dunstically set forth, & such as thought they knew as much of Gods minde as richer men, why inspiration was their ordinarie familiar, and buzde in theyr eares like a Bee in a boxe euerie houre what newes from heauen, hell, and the lands of whipperginnie, displease them who durst, hee shoulde have his mittimus to damnation *ex tempore*, they woulde vaunt there was not a pease difference twixt them and the Apostles, they were as poore as they, of as base trades as they, and no more inspired than they, and with God there is no respect of persons, onely herein may seeme some little diuersitie to lurke, that *Peter* wore a sword, and they count it flat hel fire for anie man to weare a dagger, nay so grounded and grauelled were they in this opinion, that now when they should come to battel, thers nere a one of them wold bring a blade (no not an onion blade) about him, to die for it It was not lawfull sayde they, for anie man to draw the sworde but the magistrate, and in fidelitie (which I had welnigh forgot) *Iacke Leiden* theyr magistrate had the image or likenesse of a peece of a rustie sword like a lusty lad by his side, now I remember me, it was but a foile neither, and he wore it, to shew that he should haue the foile of his enemies, which might haue bin an oracle for his twohande interpretation. *Quid plura*, his battell is pitcht, by pitcht, I do not meane set in order, for that was far from their order, onely as sailers do pitch their appareil, to make it stormeproofe, so had most of them pitcht their patcht clothes, to make them impearceable. A neerer way than to be at the charges of armor by halfe: and in another sort hee might bee sayde to haue pitcht y field, for he had pitcht or set vp his rest whither to flie if they were discomfited. Peace, peace there in the belfrie, seruice begins, vpon their knees before they ioyne, fals *Iohn Leiden* and his fraternitie verie deuoutly, they pray, they houle, they expostulate with God to grant them victory, and vse such vnspeakable vehemence, a man would thinke them the onely well bent men vtider heauen, wherein let mee dilate a little more grauely than the nature of this historie requires, or will be expected of so young a practitioner in diuinitie: that not those that intermissiuely cry, Lord open vnto us, Lord open vnto us, enter first into the kingdome of heauen, that not the greatest professors haue the greatest portion in grace, that all is not golde that glisters. When Christ sayd, the kingdome of heauen must suffer violence, hee meant not the violence of long babling praiers to no purpose, nor the violence of tedious inuective sermons without wit, but the violence of faith, the violence of good works, the violence of patient suffering. The ignorant arise and snatch the kingdome of heauen to themselues with greedines, when we with all our learning sinke downe into hell. Where did *Peter* and *Iohn* in the third of the Acts, finde the lame cripple but in the gate of the temple called beautifull, in the beautifullest gates of our temple, in the forefront of professors, are many lame cripples, lame in lyfe, lame in good workes, lame in euerie thing, yet will they alwayes sit at the gates of the temple, none be more forwarde tha they to enter into matters of reformation, yet none more behinde hand to enter into the true temple of the Lord by the gates of good life. You may obiect, that those which I speak against, are more diligent in reading the scriptures, more carefull to resort vnto sermons, more sober in their lookes and modest in their attire than anie else: but I praie you let me aunswere you, Doth not Christ saie, that before the latter daie the Sunne shall be turned into darknes, & the Moone into bloud, whereof what may the meaning be, but that the glorious sun of the gospell shall be eclipsed with the dun cloude of dissimulation, that that which is the brightest planet of saluation, shall be a meanes of errour and darknes: and the moone shal be turned into bloud, those that shine fairest, make the simplest shew, seeme most to fauour religion, shall rent out the bowels of the Church, be turned into bloud, and all this shall come to passe, before the notable daie of the Lord, whereof this age is the eue. Let me vse a more familiar example since the heate of a great number hath outraged so excessiuely. Did not the deuill leade Christ to the pinacle or highest part of the temple to tempt him, if he lead Christ, he wil leade a whole armie of hypocrites to the toppe or highest part of the temple, the highest step of religion and holines, to seduce them and subuert them. I say vnto you that which this our tempted sauiour with many other words besought his disciples, saue your selues from this froward generation. Verily, verily the seruaunt is not greater than his master: verily, verily, sinful men are not holier than holy Jesus their maker. That holy Jesus againe repeats this holy sentence, Remember the wordes I sayde vnto you, the seruant is not holier or greater than his master, as if he should say, remember then, imprint in your memorie your pride and singularitie will make you forget them, the effectes of them many yeeres hence will come to passe. Whosoeuer will seeke to saue his soule shall loose it Whosoeuer seekes by headlong meanes to enter into heauen, & disanull Gods ordinance, shal with y gyants that thought to scale heauen in contempt of Jupiter, be ouerwhelmed with mount Ossa & Pelion, & dwel with the deuill in eternal desolation. Though the high priests office was expired, when *Paul* said vnto one of them, God rebuke thee thou painted sepulchre, yet when a stander by reproued him saying, Reuilest thou the high priest? he repented & askt forgiuenesse. That which I suppose I doe not grant, the lawfulnes of the authoritie they oppose themselues agaynst, is sufficiently proued, farre bee it my vnderage argumentes should intrude themselues as a greene weake prop to support so high a building, let it suffice, if you knowe Christ, you know his father also, if you know Christianitie, you know the Fathers of the Church also, but a greate number of you with *Philip* haue bene long with Christ, and haue not knowen him, haue long professed your selues Christians, and not knowen his true ministers, you follow the French and Scotitsh fashion and faction, and in all pointes are lyke the Swizers, *Qui quorunt cum qua gente cadunt*, that seeke with what nation they may first miscarrie.

In the dayes of *Nero* there was an odde fellowe that had found out an exquisite waie to make glasse as hammer proofe as golde: shall I saie, that the like experiment he made vppon glasse, we haue practised on the Gospell? I, confidently will I, we haue found out a slight to hammer it to anie heresie whatsoeuer, but those furnaces of falshood and hammer heads of heresie must be dissolued and broken as his was, or els I feare me the false glittering glasse of innouation will bee better esteemed of than the ancient gold of the gospell. The fault of faults is this, that your dead borne faith is begotten by to too infant fathers. *Cato* one of the wisest men Roman histories canonized, was not borne till his father was foure score yeeres olde, none can be a perfect father of faith and beget men aright vnto God, but those that are aged in experience, haue many yeres imprinted in their milde conuersation, and haue with Zaclteus sold all their possessions of vanities, to inioy the sweet fellowshippe, not of the humane but spirituall messias. Ministers and pastors sell awaie your sects and schismes to the decrepite Churches in contention beyond sea, they haue bene so long inured to warre both about matters of religion and regiment, that now they haue no peace of minde, but in troubling all other mens peace. Because the pouertie of their prouinces will allow them no proportionable maintenance for higher callings of ecclesiasticall magistrates, they would reduce vs to the president of their rebellious persecuted beggerie: much like the sect of philosophers called cinikes, who when they saw they were borne to no lands or possessions, nor had anie possible meanes to support their desperate estates, but they must liue despised and in miserie doe what they could, they plotted and consulted with themselues howe to make theyr pouertie better esteemed of than rich dominion and soueraigntie. The vpshot of their plotting and consultation was this, that they would liue to themselues, scorning the verie breath or conipanie of all men, they profest (according to y rate of their lands) voluntarie pouerty, thin fare and lying hard, contemning and inueighing against al those as brute beasts whatsoeuer whom the world had giuen anie reputation for riches or prosperitie. *Diogenes* was one of the first and fonnost of the ringleaders of this rustie morositie, and he for all his nice dogged disposition, and blunt deriding of worldly drosse, and the grosse felycitie of fooles, was taken notwithstanding a little after verie fairely coining monie in his cell; so fares it vp and down with our cinicall reformed forraine Churches, they will disgest no grapes of great Bishoprikes forsooth, because they cannot tell how to come by them, they must shape their cotes good men according to their cloth, and doe as they may, not as they woulde, yet they must giue vs leaue heere in England that are their honest neighbours, if wee haue more cloth than they, to make our garment somewhat larger. What was the foundation or groundworke of this dismall declining of Munster, but the banishing of their Bishop, their confiscating and casting lots for Church liuings, as the souldiers cast lots for Christes garments, and in short tearmes, theyr making the house of God a den of theeues. The house of God a number of hungry church robbers in these dayes haue made a den of theeues. Theeues spend loosely what they haue got lightly, sacriledge is no sure inheritance, *Dionisius* was nere the richer for robbing *Iupiter* of his golden coate, he was driuen in the end to play the schoolmaster at Corinth. The name of religion, be it good or bad that is ruinated, God neuer suffers vnreuenged, He say of it as *Ouid* sayd of Eunuchs:

Qui primus pueris genitalia membra recidit Vulnera qua fecit deduit ipse pati.
   Who first depriude yong boies of their best part,   With selfe same wounds he gaue he ought to
smart.

So would he that first gelt religion or Churchliuings had bin first gelt himselfe or neuer liued, Cardinall *Wolsey* is the man I aime at, *Qui in suas ponas ingeniosus erat*, first gaue others a light to his owne ouerthrow. How it prospered with him and his instruments that after wrought for themselues, Chronicles largely report, though not apply, and some parcel of their punishment yet vnpaid, I doe not doubt but will bee required of their posteritie.

To go forward with my storie of the ouerthrowe of that vsurper *Iohn Leiden*, he and all his armie (as I saide before) falling prostrate on their faces, and ferquently giuen ouer to praier, determined neuer to cease, or leaue soliciting of God, till he had shewed them from heauen some manifest miracle of successe. Note that it was a general receiued tradition both with *I. Leiden* and all the crue of Cnipper-dolings and Muncers, if God at anie time at their vehement outcries and clamors did not condiscend to their requests, to raile on him and curse him to his face, to dispute with him, and argue him of iniustice, for not being so good as his word with them, and to vrge his many promises in the scripture against him: so that they did not serue God simply, but that hee shoulde serue their turnes, and after that tenure are many content to serue as bondmen to saue the danger of hanging: but he that serues God aright, whose vpright conscience hath for his mot, *Amor est miki causa sequendi*, I serue because I loue: he saies, *Ego te potius domine quam tua dona sequar*, He rather follow thee O Lord, for thine owne sake, than for anie couetous respect of that thou canst do for me, Christ would haue no folowers, but such as forsooke all and follow him, such as forsake all their owne desires, such as abandon all expectations of rewarde in this world, such as neglected and contemned their liues, their wiues and children in comparison of him, and were content to take vp their crosse and folow him. These Anabaptists had not yet forsooke all and followed Christ, they had not forsooke their owne desires of reuenge and innouation, they had not abandoned their expectation of the spoile of their enimies, they regarded their liues, they lookt after their wiues & children, they tooke not vp their crosse of humilitie and followed him, but would crosse him, vpbraid him, and set him at naught, if he assured not by some signe their praiers and supplications. *Deteriora sequuntur*, they folowed God as daring him. God heard their praiers, *Quod petitur poena est*, It was their speedie punishment that they praide for. Lo according to the summe of their impudent supplications, a signe in the heauens appeard the glorious signe of the rainbow, which agreed iust with the signe of their ensigne that was a rainbowe likewise. Wherevpon assuring themselues of victorie, (*Miseri quod volunt facile credunt*) that which wretches woulde haue they easily beleeue. With shoutes and clamours they presentlie ranne headlong on theyr well deserued confusion. Pittifull and lamentable was their vnpittied and well performed slaughter. To see euen a Beare (which is the most cruellest of all beastes) to too bloudily ouermatcht, and deformedly rent in peeces by an vnconscionable number of curres, it woulde moue compassion against kinde, and make those that beholding him at the stake yet vncoapte with, wisht him a sutable death to his vgly shape, now to recall their hard hearted wishes, and moane him suffering as a mild beast, in comparison of the foule mouthed mastifes his butchers: euen such compassion dyd those ouermatcht vngratious Munsterians obtayne of many indifferent eyes, who now thought them suffering, to bee as sheepe brought innocent to the shambles, when as before they deemed them as a number of wolues vp in armes agaynst the shepheardes. The Emperyalles themselues that were theyr executioners (lyke a Father that weepes when he beates his child, yet still weepes and still beates) not without much ruth and sorrow prosecuted that lamentable massacre, yet drumms and trumpets sounding nothing but stearne reuenge in their eares, made them so eager, that their hands had no leasure to aske counsell of theyr effeminate eyes, theyr swords, theyr pikes, theyr bils, their bows, their caleeuers flew, empierced, knockt downe, shot thorough, and ouerthrew as many men euerie minute of the battell, as there fais eares of corne before the sithe at one blowe, yet all theyr weapons so slaying, empiercing, knocking downe, shooting through, ouerthrowing, dissouleioyned not halfe so many, as the hailing thunder of their great ordenance so ordinary at euerie footstep was the imbrument of iron in bloud, that one could hardly discerne heads from bullettes, or clottered haire from mangled flesh hung with gore. This tale must at one time or other giue vp the ghost, and as good now as stay longer, I would gladly rid my hands of it cleanly if I could tell how, for what with talking of coblers, & tinkers, & roapemakers, and botchers, and durt-daubers, the marke is cleane gone out of my muses mouth, and I am as it were more than dunsified twixt divinitie and poetrie. What is there more as touching this tragedie that you would be resolued of? saie quickly, for now my pen is got vpon his feet again: how *I. Leiden* dide, is y it? he dide like a dog, he was hanged and the halter paid for. For his companions, do they trouble you? I can tel you they troubled some men before, for they were all kild, and none escapt, no not so much as one to tel the tale of the rainbow. Heare what it is to be Anabaptists, to bee puritans, to be villaines, you may be counted illuminate botchers for a while, but your end wil be Good people pray for me.

With the tragicall catastrophe of this munsterian conflict, did I cashier the new vocation of my caualiership. There was no more honorable wars in christendome then towards, wherefore after I had learned to be halfe an houre in bidding a man*boniure* in germane sunonimas, I trauelled along the cuntrie towards England as fast as I could. What with wagons & bare tentoes hauing attained to Middleborough (good Lord see the changing chances of vs knight arrant infants) I met with the right honourable Lord *Henrie Howard* Earle of Surrey my late master, Jesu I was perswaded.

I shoulde not be more glad to see heauen than I was to see him, O it was a right noble Lord, liberalitie itselfe, (if in this yron age there were anie such creature as liberality left on the earth) a prince in content because a Poet without peere. Destinie neuer defames her selfe but when she lets an excellent poet die: if there bee anie sparke of Adams paradized perfection yet emberd vp in the breastes of mortall men, certainely God hath bestowed that his perfectest image on poets. None come so neere to God in wit, none more contemne the world, *ratis auarus non temere est animus, sayth* Horace, *versus amat, hoc studet rnurn.* Seldom haue you seene anie Poet possessed with auarice, onely verses he loues, nothing else he delights in: and as they contemne the world, so contrarily of the mechanicall worlde are none more contemned. Despised they are of the worlde, because they are not of the world: their thoughts are exalted aboue the worlde of ignorance and all earthly conceits.

As sweet angelicall queristers they are continually conuersant in the heauen of artes, heauen it selfe is but the highest height of knowledge, he that knowes himselfe & all things else, knowes the means to be happie: happy, thrice happie are they whome God hath doubled his spirite vppon, and giuen a double soule vnto to be Poets. My heroicall master exceeded in this supernaturall kinde of wit, hee entertained no grosse earthly spirite of auarice, nor weake womanly spirit of pusillanimity and feare that are fained to be of the water, but admirable, airie, and firie spirites, full of freedome, magnanimitie and bountihood. Let me not speake anie more of his accomplishments, for feare I spend al my spirits in praising him and leaue my selfe no vigor of wit, or effectes of a soule to goe forward with my history. Hauing thus met him I so much adored, no interpleading was there of opposite occasions, but backe I must returne and beare halfe stakes with him in the lotterie of trauell.

I was not altogether vnwilling to walke along with such a good purse-bearer, yet musing what changeable humor had so sodainly seduced him from his natiue soyle to seeke out needlesse perils in these parts beyond sea, one night verie boldly I demaunded of him the reason that moued him thereto.

Ah quoth he, my little Page, full little canst thou perceiue howe farre metamorphozed I am from my selfe, since I last sawe thee. There is a little God called Loue, that will not bee worshipt of anie leaden braines, one that proclaimes himselfe sole king and Emperour of pearcing eyes and chiefe soueraigtie of softe heartes, hee it is that exercising his empire in my eyes, hath exorcized and cleane coniured me from my content. Thou knowest stately *Geraldine*, too stately I feare for me to doe homage to her statue or shrine, she it is that is come out of Italy to bewitch all the wise men of England, vpon Queene *Katherine Dowager* shee waites, that hath a dowrie of beautie sufficient to make her wooed of the greatest kings in christendome. Her high exalted sunne beames haue set the phenix neast of my breast on fire, and I my selfe haue brought Arabian spiceries of sweete passions and praises, to furnish out the funerall flame of my folly. Those who were condemned to be smothered to death by sinking downe into the softe bottome of an high built bedde of roses, neuer dide so sweete a death as I shoulde die, if her rose coloured disdaine were my deathsman. Oh thrice emperiall Hampton court, *Cupids* inchaunted castle, the place where I first sawe the perfect omnipotence of the Almightie expressed in mortalitie, tis thou alone, that tithing all other men solace in thy pleasant scituation, affoordest mee nothing but an excellent begotten sorrowe out of the chiefe treasurie of all thy recreations.

Deare *Wilton*, vnderstand that there it was where I first set eie on my more than celestiall Geraldine. Seeing her I admired her, all the whole receptacle of my sight was vnhabited with her rare worth. Long sute and vncessant protestations got me the grace to be entertained. Did neuer vnlouing seruant so prentiselike obey his neuer pleased mistres, as I dyd her. My lyfe, my wealth, my friendes, had all theyr destinie depending on her command. Uppon a time I was determined to trauell, the fame of Italy, and an especiall affection I had vnto Poetrie my second mistres, for which Italy was so famous, had wholy rauisht mee vnto it There was no dehortment from it, but needes thether I woulde, wherefore comming to my mistres as she was then walking with other Ladyes of estate in paradice at Hampton court, I most humblie besought her of fauour, that shee would giue me so much gracious leaue to absent my selfe from her seruice, as to trauell a yeare or two in Italy. She verie discreetly aunswered mee, that if my loue were so hot as I had often auouched, I dyd verie well to applie the plaister of absence vnto it, for absence, as they saie, causeth forgetfulnesse, yet neuerthelesse since it is Italy my natiue Countrie you are so desirous to see, I am the more willing to make my will yours: *I pete Italiam*, go and seeke Italie with Aenoas, but bee more true than *Aenoas*, I hope that kinde wit-cherishing climate will worke no change in so wittie a breast. No countrie of mine shall it be more, if it conspire with thee, in anie newe loue agaynst mee. One charge I will giue thee, and let it bee rather a request than a charge: When thou commest to Florence (the fayre Citie from whence I fetcht the pride of my birth) by an open challenge defende my beautie agaynst all commers.

Thou hast that honourable carryage in armes, that it shall bee no discredite for mee to bequeath all the glorie of my beautie to thy well gouerned arme. Faine woulde I be knowen where I was borne, fayne woulde I haue thee knowen where fame sits in her chiefest theater. Farewell, forget mee not, continued deserts will eternize me vnto thee, thy full wishes shall bee expired when thy trauell shall be once ended.

Heere dyd teares steppe out before wordes, and intercepted the course of my kinde concerned speech, euen as winde is allayed with raine: with heart scalding sighes I confirmed her parting request, and vowed my selfe hers, while liuing heate allowed mee to bee mine owne, *Hinc illo lachrimo* heere hence proceedeth the whole cause of my peregrination.

Not a litle was I delighted with this vnexpected loue story, especially from a mouth out of which was nought wont to march but sterne precepts of grauitie and modestie. I sweare vnto you I thought his companie the better by a thousande crownes, because he had discarded those nice tearmes of chastitie and continencie. Now I beseech God loue me so well as I loue a plain dealing man, earth is earth, flesh is flesh, earth wil to earth, and flesh vnto flesh, fraile earth, fraile flesh, who can keepe you from the worke of your creation.

23

Dismissing this fruitlesse annotation *pro et contra*, towards Venice we progrest, & tooke Roterdam in our waie, that was cleane out of our waie, there wee met with aged learninges chiefe ornament, that abundant and superingenious clarke *Erasmus*, as also with merrie sir *Thomas Moore* our Countrieman, who was come purposely ouer a little before vs, to visite the sayd graue father *Erasmus*: what talk, what conference we had then, it were heere superfluous to rehearse, but this I can assure you, *Erasmus* in al his speeches seemed so much to mislike the indiscretion of princes in preferring of parasites & fooles, that he decreed with himselfe to swim with the streame, and write a booke forthwith in commendation of folly. Quick witted sir *Thomas Moore* traueld in a cleane contrarie prouince, for hee seeing most commonwealths corrupted by ill custome, & that principalities were nothing but great piracies, which gotten by violence and murther, were maintained by priuate vndermining and bloudshed, that in the chiefest flourishing kingdomes there was no equal or wel diuided weale one with another, but a manifest conspiracie of rich men against poore men, procuring their owne vnlawfull commodities vnder the name and interest of the commonwealth: he concluded with himselfe to lay downe a perfect plot of a commonwealth or gouernment, which he would intitle his *Vtopia*. So lefte wee them to prosecute their discontented studies, & made our next iourney to Wittenberg.

At the verie point of our enterance into Wittenberg, wee were spectators of a verie solemne scolasticall entertainment of the Duke of Saxonie thether. Whome because he was the chiefe patrone of their vniuersitie, and had tooke *Luthers* parte in banishing the masse and all lyke papall Jurisdiction out of their towne, they croucht vnto extreamly. The chiefe ceremonies of their entertainment were these: first, the heads of their vniuersitie, (they were great heads of certaintie) met him in their hooded hypocrisie and doctorly accoustrement, *secundum formam statuti*, where by the Orator of the vniuersitie, whose pickerdeuant was very plentifully besprinkled with rose water, a verie learned or rather ruthfull Oration was deliuered (for it raind all the while) signifieng thus much, that it was al by patch and by peecemeale stolne out of *Tully*, & he must pardon them, though in emptying their phrase bookes, the ayre emptied his intrailes, for they did it not in anie ostentation of wit (which they had not) but to shewe the extraordinarie good will they bare the Duke, (to haue him stand in the raine tyll he was thorough wet) a thousand *quemadmodums* and *quapropters* he came ouer him with, euery sentence he concluded with *Esse posse videatur*: through all the nine worthies he ran with praising and comparing him, *Nestors* yeares hee assured him off vnder the broade seale of their supplications, and with that crowe troden verse in Virgil, *Dum iuga montis aper*, hee packt vp his pipes, and cride *dixi*.

That pageant ouerpast, there rusht vpon him a miserable rabblement of iunior graduats, that all crid out vpon him mightily in their gibrige lyke a companie of beggers, God saue your grace, God saue your grace, Jesus preserue your highnes, though it be but for an houre.

Some three halfe pennyworth of Latine here also had he throwen at his face, but it was choise stuffe I can tell you, as there is a choise euen amongest ragges gathered vp from the dunghill. At the townes end met him the burgers and dunstical incorporationers of Wittenberg in their distinguished liueries, their distinguished liuerie faces I mene, for they were most of them hot liuered dronkards, and had all the coate coulours of sanguin, purple, crimson, copper, carnation that were to be had in their countenaunces. Filthy knaues, no cost had they bestowed on the town for his welcome, sauing new painted their houghs & bousing houses, which commonly are built fayrer than their Churches, and ouer their gates set the town armes, which sounded gulping after this sort, *Vanhotten, slotten, irk bloshen glotten gelderslike*: what euer the wordes were, the sense was this, Good drinke is a medicine for all diseases.

A bursten belly inkhorne orator called *Vanderhulke* they pickt out to present him with an oration, one that had a sulpherous big swolne large face, like a Saracen, eies lyke two kentish oysters, a mouth that opened as wide euerie time hee spake, as one of those olde knit trap doores, a beard as though it had bin made of a birds neast pluckt in peeces, which consisteth of strawe, haire, and durt mixt together. Hee was apparelled in blacke leather new licourd, and a short gowne without any gathering in the backe, faced before and behind with a boistrous Beare skinne, and a red nightcap on his head. To this purport and effecte was this broccing double beere Oration.

Right noble Duke (*ideo nobilis quasi nobilis*) for you haue no bile or cholar in you, know that our present incorporation of Wittenberg, by me the tongue-man of their thankfulnes, a townesman by birth, a free Germane by nature, an oratour by arte, and a scriuener by education, in all obedience & chastity, most bountifully bid you welcome to Wittenberg: welcome sayde I? O orificiall rethorike wipe thy euerlasting mouth, and affoord me a more Indian metaphor than that, forthe braue princely bloud of a Saxon. Oratorie vncaske the hard hutch of thy complements, and with the triumphantest troupe in thy treasurie doe trewage vnto him. What impotent speech with his eight partes may not specifie this vnestimable guift holding his peace, shall as it were (with teares I speake it) do wherby as it may seeme or appeare, to manifest or declare & yet it is, & yet it is not, & yet it may bee a diminitiue oblation meritorious to your high pusillanimitie & indignity. Why shoulde I goe gadding and fisgigging after firking flantado Amphibologies, wit is wit, and good will is good will. With all the wit I haue, I here according to the premises, offer vp vnto you the Cities generall good will, which is a guilded Canne, in manner and forme following, for you and the heires of your bodie lawfully begotten, to drinke healths in. The scolasticall squitter bookes clout you vp cannopies & footclothes of verses. Wee that are good fellowes, and liue as merrie as cup and can, will not verse vpon you as they do, but must doe as we can, and entertaine you if it bee but with a playne emptie Canne. He hath learning inough that hath learnd to drinke to his first man.

Gentle Duke, without paradox be it spoken, thy horses at your owne proper costs and charges shall kneed vp to the knees all the while thou art here in spruce beere & lubeck licour. Not a dog thou bringst with thee but shall he banketted with rhenish wine and sturgion. On our shoulders we weare no lamb skin or miniuer like these academikes, yet wee can drinke to the confusion of all thy enemies. Good lambes-wooll haue we for their lambe skins, and for their miniuer, large minerals in our coffers. Mechanicall men they call vs, and not amisse, for most of vs being *Mochi*, yt is, cuckolds & whooremasters, fetch our antiquitie from the temple of *Mocha*, where Mahomet is hung vp. Three parts of the world, America, Affrike and Asia, are of this our mechanike religion. *Nero* when he crid *O quantus artifex pereo*, profest himselfe of our freedome. Insomuch as *Artifex* is a citizen or craftsman, as wel as *Carnifex* a scholler or hangman. Passe on by leaue into the precincts of our abhomination. Bony Duke, frolike in our bowse, and perswade thy selfe that euen as garlike hath three properties, to make a man winke, drinke, and stinke, so wee wyll winke on thy imperfections, drinke to thy fauorites, & all thy foes shall stinke before vs. So be it Farewell.

The Duke laught not a little at this ridiculous oration, but that verie night, as great an ironicall occasion was ministred, for he was bidden to one of the chiefe schoolesto a Comedie handled by scollers. *Acolastus* the prodigall childe was the name of it, which was so filthily acted, so leathernly sette foorth, as woulde haue moued laughter in *Heraclitus*. One as if he had beene playning a clay floore stampingly troade the stage so harde with his feete, that I thought verily he had resolued to doe the Carpenter that sette it vp some vtter shame. Another floung his armes lyke cudgelles at a peare tree, in so much as it was mightily dreaded that hee woulde strike the candles that hung aboue theyr heades out of their sockets, and leaue them all darke. Another did nothing but winke and make faces. There was a parasite, & he with clapping his hands and thripping his fingers seemed to dance an antike to and fro The onely thing they did well, was the prodigal childes hunger, most of their schollers being hungerly kept, and surely you would haue sayd they had ben brought vp in hogs academie to learne to eate acornes, if you had seene how sedulously they fell to them. Not a iest had they to keepe their auditors from sleepe but of swill and draffe, yes now and then the seruant put his hand into the dish before his master, and almost choakt himselfe, eating slouenly and rauenously to cause sport.

The next daie they had solempne disputations, where I *uther* and *Carolostadius* scolded leuell coile. A masse of words I wot well they heapt vp against the masse and the Pope, but farther perticulars of their disputations I remember not. I thought verily they woulde haue worried one another with wordes, they were so earnest and vehement. I *uther* had the louder voice, *Carolostadius* went beyond him in beating and bounsing with his fists, *Quæ supra nos nihil ad nos*. They vttered nothing to make a man laugh, therefore I wil leaue them. Mary theyr outward iestures now and then would affoorde a man a morsell of mirth: of those two I meane not so much, as of all the other traine of opponents and respondents. One peckte like a crane with his forefinger at euery halfe sillable he brought forth, and nodded with his nose like an olde singing man, teaching a yong querister to keepe time. Another would be sure to wipe his mouth with his handkercher at the end of euerie full point And euer when he thought he had cast a figure so curiously, as he diu'de ouer head and eares into his auditors admiration, hee would take occasion to stroke vp his haire, and twine vp his mustachios twice or thrice ouer while they might haue leasure to applaud him. A third wauerd and wagled his head, like a proud horse playing with his bridle, or as I haue seene some fantasticall swimmer, at euerie stroke, traine his chin sidelong ouer his left shoulder. A fourth swet and foamed at the mouth, for verie anger his aduersarie had denied that part of his sillogisme which he was not prepared to aunswere. A fifth spread his armes like an vsher that goes before to make roome, and thript with his finger & his thumbe when he thought he had tickled it with a conclusion. A sixt hung downe his countenance lyke a sheepe, and stutted and slauered verie pittifully when his inuention was stept aside out of the waie. A seuenth gaspt and gapt for winde, and groned in his pronunciation as if he were hard bound in some bad argument. Grosse plodders they were all, that had some learning and reading, but no wit to make vse of it They imagined the Duke tooke the greatest pleasure and contentment vnder heauen to heare them speak. Latine, and as long as they talkt nothing but *Tully* he was bound to attend them. A most vaine thing it is in many vniuersities at this daye, that they count him excellent eloquent, who stealeth not whole phrases but whole pages out of *Tully*. If of a number of shreds of his sentences he can shape an oration, from all the world hee carries it awaie, although in truth it be no more than a fooles coat of many coulours. No inuention or matter haue they of theyr owne, but tacke vp a stile of his stale galimafries. The leaden headed Germanes first began this, and we Englishmen haue surfetted of their absurd imitation. I pittie *Nizolius* that had nothing to doe, but picke thrids ends out of an olde ouerworne garment. This is but by the waie, we must looke backe to our disputants. One amongst the rest thinking to be more conceited than his fellowes, seeing the Duke haue a dog hee loued well, which sate by him on the tarras, conuerted all his oration to him, and not a haire of his taile but he kembd out with comparisons. So to haue courted him if he were a bitch had bin verie suspitious. Another commented & descanted on the Dukes staffe, new tipping it with many queint epithites. Some cast his natiuitie, and promised him he should not die till the daie of Iudgement Omitting further superfluities of this stampe, in this general assembly we found intermixed that abundant scholler *Cornelius Agrippa*. At that time he bare the fame to be the greatest coniurer in Christendome. *Scoto* that did the iugling trickes here before the Queene, neuer came neere him one quarter in magicke reputation. The Doctors of Wittenberg doting on the rumour that went of him, desired him before the Duke and them to doe something extraordinarie memorable.

One requested to see pleasant *Plautus*, & that he would shew them in what habite hee went, and with what countenaunce he lookt, when he ground corne in the mill. Another had halfe a moneths minde to *Ouid* and his hooke nose. *Erasmus* who was not wanting to that honourable meeting, requested to see *Tully* in that same grace and maiestie he pleaded his Oration *pro Roscio Amerino*. Affirming, that til in person he beheld his importunitie of pleading, he woulde not be perswaded anie man coulde carrie awaie a manifest case with rethorike, so straungely. To *Erasmus* petition he easily condiscended, and willing the Doctours at such an houre to holde theyr conuocation, and euerie one to keepe him in his place without mouing: at the time prefixed in entered *Tully*, ascended his pleading place, and declaimed verbatim the fornamed Oration, but with such astonishing amazement, with such feruent exaltation of spirite, with such soule-stirring iestures, that all his auditours were readie to install his guiltie client for a God.

Greate was the concourse of glorie *Agrippa* drewe to him with this one feate. And in deede hee was so cloyed with men which came to beholde him, that hee was fayne sooner than hee woulde, to returne to the Emperours court from whence he came, and leaue Wittenberg before hee woulde. With him we trauelled along, hauing purchast his acquaintance a little before. By the waie as wee went, my master and I agreed to change names. It was concluded betwixte vs, that I shoulde bee the Earle of Surrie, and hee my man, onely because in his owne person, which hee woulde not haue reproched, he meant to take more libertie of behauiour. As for my carryage hee knew hee was to tune it at a key, eyther high or low, or as hee list.

To the Emperours Court wee came, where our entertainment was euerie waie plentifull, carouses wee had in whole galons in stead of quart pots. Not a health was giuen vs but contayned well ncere a hogshead. The customes of the Countrie we were eager to be instructed in, but nothing we coulde learne but this, that euer at the Emperours coronation there is an Oxe roasted with a stagge in the belly, and that stagge in his belly hath a kidde, and that kidde is stufte full of birdes. Some courtiers to wearie out time woulde tell vs further tales of *Cornelius Agrippa*, and how when sir *Thomas Moore* our countrieman was there, hee shewed him the whole destruction of Troy in a dreame. How the Lorde *Cromwell* being the kings Embassador there, in lyke case, in a perspectiue glasse he set before his eyes, King Henrie the eight with all his Lordes hunting in his forrest at Windsore, and when he came into his studie, and was verie vrgent to be partaker of some rare experiment, that he might report when he came into England, he wilde him amongst two thousande great bookes to take downe which he list, and begin to reade one line in anie place, and without booke he woulde rehearse twentie leaues following. *Cromwell* dyd so, and in manye bookes tride him, when in euerie thing hee exceeded his promise and conquered his expectation. To *Charles* the fifte then Emperour, they reported how he shewed the nine worthies, *Dauid, Salomon, Gedeon*, and the rest, in that similitude and lykenesse that they liued vpon earth. My master and I hauing by the high waie side gotten some reasonable familiaritie with him, vpon this accesse of myracles imputed to him, resolued to request him something in our owne behalfes. I because I was his suborned Lorde and master, desired him to see the liuely image of *Geraldine* his loue in the glasse, and what at that instant she did, and with whome shee was talking. Hee shewed her vs without more adoe, sicke weeping on her bedde, and resolued all into deuoute religion for the absence of her Lorde. At the sight thereof hee coulde in no wise refrayne, though hee had tooke vppon him the condition of a seruant, but hee must forthwith frame this extemporall Dittie.

All soule, no earthly fleshy why dost thou fade,   All gold, no worthlesse drosse, why lookst thou pale,   Sicknesse how darst thou one so faire inuadey   Too base infirmitie to worke her bale, Heauen be distemperd since she grieuedpines,   Neuer be drie these my sadplaintiue lines.   Pearch thou my spirit on her siluer breasts,   And with theirpaine redoubled musike beatings,   Let them tosse thee to world where all toile rests,   Where blisse is subiect to nofeares defeatings,   Her praise I tune whose tongue doth tune the sphears,   And gets new muses in her hearers eares.   Starres fall to fetch fresh light from her rich eyes,   Her bright brow driues the Sunne to clouds beneath,   Her hair es reflexe with red strokes paints the skies,   Sweet morne and euening deaw flowes from her breath: Phoebe rules tides, she my teares tides forth drawesy   In her sicke bed hue sits and maketh lawes.   Her daintie limbes tinsel I her silke soft sheets,   Her rose-crownd cheekes eclipse my daze led sight,   O glasse with too much ioy my thoughts thou greets,   And yet thou shewst me day but by twielight   Ile kisse thee for the kindnesse I hauefelt,   Her lips one kisse would vnto Nectar melt.

Though the Emperors court, and the extraordinaire edifieng companie of *Cornelius Agrippa* might haue beene arguments of waight to haue arested vs a little longer there, yet Italy stil stuck as a great moat in my masters eie, he thought he had trauelled no farther tha Wales til he had tooke suruey of that Countrie which was such a curious moulder of wits.

To cut off blinde ambages by the high way side, we made a long stride & got to Venice in short time, where hauing scarce lookt about vs, a precious supernaturall pandor, apparelled in all points like a gentleman, and hauing halfe a dosen seuerall languages in his purse, entertained vs in our owne tongue verie paraphrastically and eloquently, and maugre all other pretended acquaintance, would haue vs in a violent kinde of curtesie to be the guests of his appointment. His name was *Petro de campo Frego*, a notable practitioner in the pollicy of baudrie. The place whether he brought vs, was a pernicious curtizans house named *Tabitha* the Temptresses, a wench that could set as ciuill a face on it, as chastities first martyr *Lucrecia*. What will you conceit to bee in anie Saintes house that was there to seeke? Bookes, pictures, beades, crucifixes, why there was a haberdashers shop of them in euerie chamber. I warrant you should not see one set of her neckercher peruerted or turned awrie, not a piece of a haire displast. On her beddes there was not a wrinkle of anie wallowing to be founde, her pillowes bare out as smooth as a groning wiues belly, & yet she was a Turke and an infidell, and had more dooinges than all her neighbours besides. Us for our money they vsed lyke Emperours, I was master as you hearde before, and my master the Earle was but as my chiefe man whome I made my companion. So it happened (as iniquitie will out at one time or other) that she perceiuing my expence had no more ventes than it should haue, fell in with my supposed semant my man, and gaue him halfe a promise of marriage, if he woulde helpe to make me away, that she and he might inioy the iewels and wealth that I had.

The indifficultie of the condition thus she explaind vnto him, her house stood vpon vaults, which in two hundred yeeres together were neuer searcht, who came into her house none tooke notice of, his fellow seruants that knewe of his masters abode there, should be all dispatcht by him as from his master, into sundrie partes of the citie about busines, and when they returned, answere should bee made that hee lay not there anie more, but had remoued to Padua since their departure, & thether they must follow him. Now (quoth she) if you be disposed to make him awaie in their absence, you shall haue my house at command. Stab, poison, or shoote him through with a pistol all is one, into the vault he shall be throwen when the deede is done. On my bare honestie it was a craftie queane, for she had enacted with her selfe if he had bin my legitimate seruant, as he was one that serued and supplied my necessities, when hee had murthered me, to haue accused him of the murther, and made all that I had hers (as I carryed all my masters wealth, monie, iewels, rings, or bils of exchaunge continually about me.) He verie subtilly consented to her stratageme at the first motion, kill me he woulde, that heauens could not withstand, and a pistoll was the predestinate engin which must deliuer the parting blow. God wot I was a rawe young squier, and my master dealt iudasly with me, for he tolde mee but euerie thing that she and he agreed of. Wherfore I could not possibly preuent it, but as a man woulde saie auoide it. The execution daie aspired to his vtmost deuolution, into my chamber came my honourable attendant with his pistoll charged by his side verie suspitiously and sullenly, lady *Tabitha* and *Petro de catnpo Frego* her pandor followed him at the hard heeles. At theyr enterance I saluted them all verie familiarly and merily, and began to impart vnto them what disquiet dreames had disturbed me the last night I dreamd, quoth I, that my man *Brunquell* heere (for no better name got he of mee) came into my chamber with a pistoll charged vnder his arme to kill me, and that hee was suborned by you mistres *Tabitha*, and my verie good friend here *Petro de campo Frego*. God send it tourne to good, for it hath afrighted mee aboue measure. As they were readie to enter into a colourable common place of the deceitful friuolousnes of dreames, my trustie seruant *Brunquell* stoode quiuering and quaking euerie ioynt of him, and (as it was before compacted between vs) let his pistoll drop from him on the sodain, wherwith I started out of my bed, and drew my rapier and cride murther, murther, which made good wife *Tabitha* readie to bepisse her.

My seruant, or my master, which you will, I tooke roughly by the coller, and threatned to run him thorough incontinent if he confest not the truth. He as it were striken with remorse of conscience (God be with him, for he could counterfeit most daintily) downe on his knees, askt me forgiuenes, and impeached *Tabitha* and *Petro de catnpo Frego* as guiltie of subornation. I verie mildly and grauely gaue him audience, raile on them I did not after his tale was ended, but sayd I would trie what the lawe coulde doe. Conspiracie by the custome of their countrie was a capitall offence, and what custome or iustice might affoord they should be all sure to feele. I could (quoth I) acquite my selfe otherwise, but it is not for a straunger to bee his owne caruer in reuenge. Not a worde more with *Tabitha* but die she would before God or the deuill would haue her, she sounded and reuiued, and then sounded againe, and after shee reuiued again sighed heauily, spoke faintly and pittifully, yea and so pittifully, as if a man had not knowen the prankes of harlots before, he would haue melted in comiseration. Tears, sighs, and dolefull tuned wordes could not make anie forcible claime to my stonie eares, it was the glistering crownes that I hungered and thirsted after, and with them for all her mock holyday iestures she was faine to come off, before I woulde condiscend to anie bargaine of silence. So it fortuned (fie vpon that vnfortunate word of Fortune) yt this whore, this quean, this curtizan, this common of ten thousand, so bribing me not to bewray her, had giuen me a great deale of counterfeit gold, which she had receiued of a coiner to make awaie a little before. Amongst the grosse summe of my briberie, I silly milkesop mistrusting no deceit, vnder an angell of light tooke what she gaue me, nere turnd it ouer, for which (O falsehood in faire shew) my master and I had like to haue bin turned ouer. Hee that is a knight arrant, exercised in the affaires of Ladies and Gentlewomen, hath more places to send mony to, than the diuell hath to send his spirites to. There was a delicate wench called *Flauia Aemilia* lodging in S. Markes streete at a Goldsmiths, which I would faine haue had to the grand test, to trie whether she were currant in alcumie or no. Aie me, shee was but a counterfeit slip, for she not only gaue me the slip, but had welnie made me a slipstring. To her I sent my gold to beg an hour of grace, ah gracelesse fornicatresse, my hostesse & she wer confederate, who hauing gotten but one piece of my ill golde into their kandes, deuised the meanes to make me immortall. I could drinke for anger till my head akt, to think how I was abused. Shall I shame the deuill and speake the truth, to prison was I sent as principall, and my master as accessarie, nor was it to a prison neither, but to the master of the mints house who though partly our iudge, and a most seuere vpright iustice in his own nature, extreamly seemed to condole our ignorant estate, and without all peraduenture a present redresse he had ministred, if certaine of our countrie men hearing an English earle was apprehended for coining, had not come to visite vs. An ill planet brought them thether, for at the first glance they knew the seruant of my secrecies to be the Earle of Surrey, and I (not worthie to be named I) an outcast of his cup or his pantofles. Thence, thence sprong the full period of our infelicitie. The master of the mint our whilome refresher and consolation, now tooke part against vs, he thought we had a mint in our head of mischieuous conspiracies against their state. Heauens bare witnes with vs it was not so, (Heauens wyll not always come to witnes when they are cald.)

To a straiter ward were we comitted: that which we haue imputatiuely transgressed must beaunswered. O the heathen heigh passe, and the intrinsccall legerdemain of our special approued good pandor *Petro de Campo Frego*. Hee although he dipt in the same dish with vs euerie daie, seeming to labor our cause verie importunatly, and had interpreted for vs to the state from y beginning, yet was one of those trecherous brother *Trulies*, and abused vs most darkly. He interpreted to vs with a pestilence, for whereas we stood obstinatly vpon it, we were wrongfully deteined, and that it was naught but a malicious practise of sinfull *Tabitha* our late hostesse, he by a fine conny-catching corrupt translation, made vs plainely to confesse, and crie *Miserere*, ere we had need of our neckverse.

Detestable, detestable, that the flesh and the deuill shoulde deale by their factors. He stand to it, there is not a pandor but hath vowed paganisme. The deuill himselfe is not such a deuill as he, so be he performe his function aright. He must haue the backe of an asse, the snout of an elephant, the wit of a foxe, and the teeth of a wolfe, he must faune like a spaniell, crouch like a Jew, Here like a sheepbiter. If he be halfe a puritan, and haue scripture continually in his mouth, he speeds the better. I can tell you it is a trade of great promotion, and let none euer thinke to mount by seruice in forain courts, or creep neere to some magnifique Lords, if they be not seene in this science. O it is the art of arts, and ten thousand times goes beyond the intelligencer. None but a staid graue ciuill man is capable of it, he must haue exquisite courtship in him or else he is not old who, he wants the best point in his tables.

God be mercifull to our pandor (and that were for God to worke a miracle) he was seene in all the seuen liberall deadly sciences, not a sinne but he was as absolute in as sathan himselfe. Sathan could neuer haue supplanted vs so as hee did. I may saie to you he planted in vs the first Italionate wit that we had. During the time we lay close and toke phisick in this castle of contemplation, there was a Magnificos wife of good calling sent in to beare vs companie. Her husbands name was *Castaldo*, she hight *Diamante*, the cause of her committing was an vngrounded ielous suspition which her doating husbande had conceiued of her chastitie. One *Isaac Medicus* a bergomast was the man hee chose to make him a monster, who beeing a courtier and repairing to his house very often, neither for loue of him nor his wife, but onely with a drift to borrowe monie of a pawne of waxe and parchment, when he sawe his expectation deluded, and that *Castaldo* was too charie for him to close with, he priuily with purpose of reuenge, gaue out amongst his copesmates, that hee resorted to *Castaldos* house for no other end but to cuckolde him, & doubtfully he talkt that he had and he had not obtained his sute. Rings which he borrowed of a light curtizan that he vsed to, hee woulde faine to bee taken from her fingers, and in summe, so handled the matter, that *Castaldo* exclaimd, Out whore, strumpet, sixe penny hackster, away with her to prison.

As glad were we almost as if they had giuen vs libertie, that fortune lent vs such a sweet puefellow. A pretie round faced wench was it, with blacke cie browes, a high forehead, a litle mouth, and a sharpe nose, as fat and plum euerie part of her as a plouer, a skin as slike and soft as the backe of a swan, it doth me good when I remember her. Like a birde she tript on the ground, and bare out her belly as maiesticall as an Estrich. With a licorous rouling eie fixt percing on the earth, & sometimes scornfully darted on the tone side, she figured foorth a high discontented disdain, much like a prince puffing and storming at the treason of some mightie subiect fled lately out of his power. Her verie countenance repiningly wrathfull, and yet cleere and vnwrinkled, would haue confirmed the cleernes of her conscience to the austerest iudge in the world. If in any thing she were culpable, it was in being too melancholy chast, and shewing her selfe as couetous of her beautie as her husband was of his bags. Many are honest because they knowe not how to be dishonest: she thought there was no pleasure in stolne bread, because there was no pleasure in an olde mans bed. It is almost impossible that anie woman should be excellently wittie, and not make the vtmost pennie of her beautie. This age and this countrie of ours admits of some miraculous exceptions, but former times are my constant informers. Those that haue quicke motions of wit, haue quicke motions in euerie thing: yron onely needes many strokes, onely yron wits are not wonne without a long siege of intreatie. Golde easily bends, the most ingenious mindes are easiest moued,*Ingenium nobis molle Thalia dedit*, saith *Psapho* to *Phao*. Who hath no mercifull milde mistres, I will maintaine, hath no wittie but a clownish dull flegmatike puppie to his mistres.

This Magnificos wife was a good louing soule, that had mettall inough in her to make a good wit of, but being neuer remoued from vnder her mothers and her husbands wing, it was not moulded and fashioned as it ought. Causelesse distrust is able to driue deceite into a simple womans head. I durst pawne the credit of a page, which is worth ams ase at all times, that she was immaculate honest till she met with vs in prison. Marie what temptations shee had then when fire and flaxe were put together, conceit with your selues, but hold my master excusable.

Alacke he was too vertuous to make her vicious, he stoode vpon religion and conscience, what a hainous thing it was to subuert Gods ordinance. This was all the iniurie he woulde offer her, sometimes he woulde imagine her in a melancholic humour to be his *Geraldine*, and court her in tearmes correspondent, nay he would sweare shee was his *Geraldine*, & take her white hand and wipe his eyes with it, as though the very touch of her might stanch his anguish. Now would he kneele and kisse the ground as holy grounde which she vouchsafed to blesse from barrennesse by her steps. Who loueth learned to write an excellent passion, might have bin a perfect tragicke poet, had he but attended halfe the extremitie of his lament. Passion vpon passion would throng one on anothers necke, he would praise her beyond the moone and starres, and that so sweetly & rauishingly, as I perswade myself he was more in loue with his owne curious forming fancie than her face, and truth it is, many become passionate louers, only to win praise to theyr wits.

He praised, he praied, hee desired and besought her to pittie him that perisht for her. From this his intranced mistaking extasie could no man remoue him. Who loueth resolutely, will include euerie thing vnder the name of his loue. From prose he would leape into verse, and with these or such lyke rimes assault her.

If I must die, O let me choose my death,   Sucke out my soule with kisses cruell maide,   In thy breasts christall bals enbalme my breath,   Dole it all out in sighs when I am laid.   Thy lips on mine like cupping glasses claspe,   Let our tongs meete and siriue as they would sting,   Crush out my winde with one strait girting graspe,   Stabs on my heart keepe time whitest thou dost sing.   Thy eies like searingyrons burne out mine,   In thy faire tresses stifle me outright,   Like Circes change me to a loathsome swine,   So I may liue for euer in thy sight   Into heauens ioyes can none prof oundly see, Except that first they meditate on thee.

Sadly and verily, if my master said true, I should if I were a wench make many men quickly immortall. What ist, what ist for a maide fayre and freshe to spend a little lip salue on a hungrie louer. My master beate the bush and kept a coile and a pratling, but I caught the birde, simplicitie and plainnesse shall carrie it awaie in another world. God wot he was *Petro Desperato,* when I stepping to hir with a dunstable tale made vp my market A holy requiem to their soules that thinke to wooe women with riddles. I had some cunning plot you must suppose, to bring this about Her husband had abused her, and it was verie necessarie she shoulde be reuenged. Seldome doe they proue patient martyrs who are punisht vniustly. One way or other they wil cry quittance whatsoeuer it cost them. No other apte meanes had this poore shee captiued *Cicely,* to worke her hoddy peake husbande a proportionable plague to his ielousie, but to giue his head his ful loding of infamie. She thought she would make him complaine for some thing, that now was so hard bound with an hereticall opinion. Howe I dealt with her, gesse gentle reader, *Sub audi* that I was in prison, and she was my Jailor.

Meanes there was made after a moneths or two durance by M. *Iohn Russell,* a gentleman of king Henrie the eights chamber, who then lay lieger at *Venice* for England, that our cause should be fauorably heard. At that time was Monsieur *Petro Aretino* searcher and chiefe Inquisiter for the colledge of curtizans. Diuerse and sundrie wayes was this *Aretine* beholding to the king of England, especially for by this foresaid M. *Russell* a little before he had sent him a pension of foure hundreth crownes yerely during his life. Very forcibly was hee dealt withall, to straine the vtmost of his credit for our deliuerie. Nothing at his handes wee sought, but that the curtizan might be more narrowly sifted and examined. Such and so extraordinarie was his care and industrie heerein, that within few dayes after mistres *Tabitha* and her pandor cride *Peccaui confiteor,* and we were presently discharched, they for example sake executed. Most honorably after our enlargement of the state were we vsed, and had sufficient recompence for all our troubles and wrongs.

Before I goe anie further, let me speake a word or two of this *Aretine.* It was one of the wittiest knaues that euer God made. If out of so base a thing as inke there may be extracted a spirite, he writ with nought but the spirite of inke, and his stile was the spiritualtie of artes, and nothing else, where as all others of his age were but the lay temporaltie of inkhorne tearmes. For in deede they were meere temporizers, & no better. His penne was sharpe pointed like ponyard. No leafe he wrote on, but was like a burning glasse to sette on fire all his readers. With more then musket shot did he charge his quill, where he meant to inueigh. No one houre but he sent a whole legion of deuils into some heard of swine or other. If *Martiall* had ten muses (as he sayth of himselfe) when hee but tasted a cup of wine, he had ten score when he determined to tyranize. Nere a line of his but was able to make a man dronken with admiration. His sight pearst like lightning into the intrailes of al abuses. This I must needs saie, that most of his learning hee gotte by hearing the lectures at Florence. It is sufficient that learning he had, and a conceite exceeding all learning, to quintescence euerie thing which he hard. He was no timerous seruile flatterer of the commonwealth wherein he liued. His tongue and his inuention were foreborne, what they thought they would confidently vtter. Princes hee sparde not, that in the least point transgrest. His life he contemned in comparison of the libertie of speech. Whereas some dull braine maligners of his, accuse him of that treatise *de tribus impostoribus Mundi,* which was neuer contriued without a generall counsell of deuils, I am verily perswaded it was none of his, and of my minde are a number of the most iudiciall Italians. One reason is this, because it was published fortie yeeres after his death, and he neuer in all his life wrote anie thing in Latine. Certainly I haue heard that one of *Machiuuels* followers and disciples was the author of that booke, who to auoid discredite, filcht it forth vnder *Aretines* name, a great while after hee had sealed vp his eloquent spirit in the graue. Too much gall dyd that wormwood of Gibeline wits put in his inke, who ingraued that rubarbe Epitaph on this excellent Poets tombstone, Quite forsaken of all good Angels was he, and vtterly giuen ouer to an artlesse enuie. Foure vniuersities honored *Aretine* with these rich titles, *Il flagello de principe Il veritiero, Il deuino, & Lvnico Aretino.* The French king Frances the first, he kept in such awe, that to chaine his tongue, he sent him a huge chaine of golde, in the forme of tongues fashioned. Singularly hath hee commented of the humanity of Christ Besides, as Moses set forth his Genesis, so hath hee set forth his Genesis also, including the contents of the whole Bible. A notable treatise hath hee compiled, called *Il sette Psalmi ponetentiarii.* All the *Thomasos* haue cause to loue him, because he hath dilated so magnificently of the life of Saint Thomas.

There is a good thing that he hath set forth *La vita della virgine Maria*, though it somewhat smell of superstition, with a number more, which here for tediousnesse I suppresse. If lasciuious he were, he may answere with *Ouid, Vita verecunda est, musa iocosa mea est*, My lyfe is chast though wanton be my verse. Tell mee who is most trauelled in histories, what good Poet is or euer was there, who hath not had a little spice of wantonnes in dayes? Euen *Beza* himselfe by your leaue. *Aretine* as long as the worlde liues shalt thou liue. *Tully, Virgil, Ouid, Seneca*, were neuer such ornaments to Italy as thou hast beene. I neuer thought of Italy more religiously than England til I heard of thee. Peace to thy Ghost, and yet mee thinkes so indefinite a spirite should haue no peace or intermission of paines, but be penning Ditties to the Archangels in another world. Puritans spue forth the venome of your dull inuentions. A Toade swelles with thicke troubled poison, you swell with poisonous perturbations, your mallice hath not a cleare dram of anie inspired disposition.

My principall subiect pluckes me by the elbowe, *Diamante Castaldos* the magnificos wife, after my enlargment proued to bee with childe, at which instant there grewe an vnsatiable famine in Venice, wherein, whether it were for meere niggardise, or that *Castaldo* still eate out his heart with iealousie, Saint Anne be our recorde, he turnde vp the heeles verie deuoutly. To master *Aretine* after this, once more verie dutifully I appeald, requested him of fauour, acknowledged former gratuities, hee made no more humming or haulting, but in despite of her husbandes kinsfolkes, gaue her her *Nunc dimittis*, and so establisht her free of my companie.

Beeing out, and fully possest of her husbandes goods, she inuested mee in the state of a Monarch. Because the time of childbirth drew nigh, and shee coulde not remaine in Venice but discredited, she decreed to trauell whether so euer I woulde conduct her. To see Italy throughout was my proposed scope, and that waie if shee woulde trauell, haue with her, I had wherewithall to relieue her.

From my master by her fulhand prouokement I parted without leaue, the state of an Earle hee had thrust vppon me before, and nowe I woulde not bate him an inch of it. Through all the Cities past I by no other name but the yong Earle of Surrey, my pompe, my appareil, traine, and expence, was nothing inferiour to his, my lookes were as loftie, my wordes as magnificall. Memorandum, that Florence beeing the principall scope of my masters course, missing mee, he iourneied thether without interruption. By the waie as he went, he heard of another Earle of Surrey besides himselfe, which caused him make more hast to fetch me in, whom he little dreamed of, had such art in my budget, to separate the shadowe from the bodie.

Ouertake me at Florence he did, where sitting in my pontificalibus with my curtizan at supper, lyke *Anthonie and Cleopatra*, when they quafte standing bowles of wine spiced with pearle together, he stole in ere we sent for him, and bad much good it vs, and askt vs whether we wanted anie guests. If he had askt me whether I would haue hanged my selfe, his question had beene more acceptable. He that had then vngartered mee, might haue pluckt out my heart at my hams.

My soule which was made to soare vpward, now sought for passage downward, my blood as the blushing *Sabine* maids surprized on the sodain by the souldiers of *Romulus*, ran to the noblest of bloud amongest them for succour, that were in no lesse (if not greater daunger) so dyd it runne for refuge to the noblest of his bloude about my heart assembled that stood in more need it selfe of comfort and refuge. A trembling earthquake or shaking feauer assailed either of vs, and I thinke vnfainedly, if he seeing our faint heart agonie, had not soone cheered and refreshed vs, the dogs had gone together by the eares vnder the table for our feare-dropped lims.

In stead of menacing or afrighting me with his swoord, or his frounes for my superlatiue presumption, hee burst out into a laughter aboue Ela, to thinke how brauely napping hee had tooke vs, and how notablie wee were dampt & stroke dead in the neast, with the vnexpected view of his presence.

Ah quoth he, my noble Lord, (after his tongue had borrowed a little leaue of his laughter) is it my lucke to visite you thus vnlookt for, I am sure you wil bid me welcome, if it be but for the names sake. It is a wonder to see two English Earles of one house, at one time together in Italy. I hearing him so pleasant, began to gather vp my spirits, and replide as boldly as I durst Sir, you are welcome, your name which I haue borrowed I haue not abused. Some large summes of money this my sweete mistres *Diamante* hath made me master of, which I knew not how better to imploy for the honour of my country, than by spending it munificently vnder your name. No Englishman would I haue renowmed for bounty, magnificence and curtesie but you, vnder your colours all my meritorious workes I was desirous to shroud. Deeme it no insolence to adde increase to your fame. Had I basely and beggerly, wanting abilitie to support anie parte of your roialtie, vndertooke the estimation of this high calling, your alledgement of iniury had ben the greater, and my defence lesse authorized. It will be thought but a policie of yours thus to send one before you, who being a follower of yours, shall keepe and vphold the estate and port of an Earle. I haue knowen many Earles my selfe that in their owne persons would go verie plaine, but delighted to haue one that belonged to them (being loden with iewels, apparelled in cloth of golde and all the rich imbroderie that might bee) to stand bare headed vnto him, arguing thus much, that if y greatest men went not more sumptuous, how more great than the greatest was he that could command one going so sumptuous. A noble mans glorie appeareth in nothing so much as in the pompe of his attendants. What is the glorie of the Sunne, but that the moone and so many millions of starres borrow their light from him? If you can reprehend me of anie one illiberall licentious action I haue disparaged your name with, heape shame on me prodigally, I beg no pardon or pittie. *Non reniunt in idem pudor & amor,* hee was loth to detract from one that he loued so. Beholding with his eies that I dipt not the wings of his honor, but rather increast them with additions of expence, he intreated me as if I had bin an Embassadour, he gaue me his hand and swore he had no more hearts but one, and I should haue halfe of it, in that I so inhanced his obscured reputation. One thing, quoth he, my sweete Jacke I will intreate thee (it shalbe but one) that though I am wel pleased thou shouldest be the ape of my birthright, (as what noble man hath not his ape & his foole) yet that thou be an ape without a clog, not carrie thy curtizan with thee. I tolde him that a king could do nothing without his treasury, this curtizan was my purs-bearer, my countenance and supporter. My earldome I would sooner resigne than part with such a speciall benefactresse. Resigne it I will how euer, since I am thus challenged of stolne goods by the true owner: Lo, into my former state I returne againe, poore *Iack Wilton* and your seruant am I, as I was at the beginning, and so will I perseuer to my liues ending.

That theame was quickly cut off, and other talke entered in place, of what I haue forgot, but talke it was, and talke let it be, and talke it shall be, for I do not meane here to remember it. We supt, we got to bed, we rose in the morning, on my master I waited, and the first thing he did after he was vp, he went and visited the house where his *Geraldine* was borne, at sight wherof he was so impassioned, that in the open street but for me, he would haue made an oration in praise of it. Into it we were conducted, and shewed each seuerall roome therto appertaining. O but when he came to the chamber where his *Geraldines* cleere Sunbeams first thrust themselues into this cloude of flesh, and acquainted mortalitie with the puritie of Angels, then did his mouth ouerflowe with magnificats, his tongue thrust the starres out of heauen, and eclipsed the Sun and Moone with comparisons, *Geraldine* was the soule of heauen, sole daughter and heire to *primus motor.* The alcumy of his eloquence, out of the incomprehensible drossie matter of clouds and aire, distilled no more quintescence than woulde make his Geraldine compleat faire.

In praise of the chamber that was so illuminatiuely honoured with her radiant conception, he penned this sonet:

Faire rootne the presence of sweet beauties pride,   *The place the Sunne vpon the earth did hold, When Phaton his chariot did misguide,*   *The towre where loue raind downe himselfe in gold.*   *Prostrate as holy groutid He worship thee,*   *Our Ladies chappell henceforth be thou nanid.*   *Heere first loues Queene put on mortalitie,*   *And with her beautie all the world inflamed.*   *Heatfns chambers harboring firie cherubines,*   *Are not with thee in glorie to compare,*   *Lightning it is not light which in thee shines, None enter thee but straight entranced are.*   *O if Elizium be aboue the ground,*   *Then here it is where nought but ioy is found.*

Many other Poems and Epigrams in that chambers patient alablaster inclosure (which her melting eies long sithence had softned) were curiously ingraued. Diamondes thought themselues *Dii mundi,* if they might but carue hir name on the naked glasse. With them on it did he anatomize these bodie-wanting mots, *Dulce puella malum est. Quod fugit ipse sequor. Amor est teni causa sequendi. O infolix ego. Cur vidi, curperii. Non patienter amo. Tantum patiatur amari.* After the viewe of these veneriall monumentes, he published a proude challenge in the Duke of Florence court agaynst all commers, (whether Christians, Turkes, Canibals, Jewes, or Saracens), in defence of his Geraldines beautie. More mildly was it accepted, in that she whom he defended, was a towne borne child of that Citie, or else the pride of the Italian would haue preuented him ere he should haue come to performe it. The Duke of Florence neuerthelesse sent for him, and demanded him of his estate, and the reason that drew him thereto, which when hee was aduertised of to the full, he granted all Countries whatsoeuer, as wel enemies and outlawes, as friendes and confederates, free accesse and regresse into his dominions vnmolested, vntill that insolent triall were ended.

The right honourable and euer renowmed Lorde *Henrie Howard* Earle of Surrey my singular good Lorde and master, entered the listes after this order. His armour was all intermixed with lyllies and roses, and the bases therof bordered with nettles and weeds, signifieng stings, crosses, and ouergrowing incumbrances in his loue, his helmet round proportioned like a gardeners waterpot, from which seemed to issue forth small thrids of water, like citerne stringes, that not only did moisten the lillies and roses, but did fructifie as well the nettles and weedes, and made them ouergrow their liege Lordes. Whereby hee did importe thus much, that the teares that issued from his braine, as those arteficiall distillations issued from the well counterfeit waterpot on his head, watered and gaue life as well to his mistres disdaine (resembled to nettles and weedes) as increase of glorie to her care-causing beautie, (comprehended vnder the lillies and roses.) The simbole thereto annexed was this, *ex lachrimis lachrimæ.* The trappings of his horse were pounced and boulstered out with rough plumed siluer plush, in full proportion and shape of an Estrich. On the breast of the horse were the forepartes of this greedie birde aduaunced, whence as his manner is, hee reacht out his long necke to the raines of the bridle, thinking they had beene yron, and styll seemed to gape after the golden bit, and euer as the courser dyd rayse or curuet, to haue swallowed it halfe in. His winges, which hee neuer vseth but running, beeing spreaded full sayle, made his lustie steede as proude vnder him as he had beene some other *Pegasus*, and so quieueringly and tenderly were these his broade wings bound to either side of him, that as he paced vp and downe the tilt-yard in his maiestie ere the knights were entered, they seemed wantonly to fan in his face and make a flickering sound, such as Eagles doe, swiftly pursuing their praie in the ayre. On either of his winges, as the Estrich hath a sharpe goade or pricke wherewith hee spurreth himselfe forwarde in his saile-assisted race, so this artificiall Estrich, on the imbent knuckle of the pinion of either wing, had embossed christall eies affixed, wherein wheele wise were circularly ingrafted sharpe pointed diamonds, as rayes from those eies deriued, that like the rowels of a spurre ran deep into his horse sides, and made him more eager in his course.

Such a fine dimme shine dide these christall eies and these round enranked diamonds make through their bolne swelling bowres of feathers, as if it had beene a candle in a paper lanterne, or a gloworme in a bush by night, glistering through the leaues and briers. The taile of the Estrich being short and thicke, serued verie fitly as a plume to tricke vp his horse taile with, so that euerie parte of him was as naturally coapted as might be. The word to this deuice was *Aculeo alatus,* I spread my wings onely spurd with her eies. The morral of the whole is this, that as the Estrich, the most burning sighted bird of all others, insomuch as the female of them hatcheth not hir egs by couering them, but by the effectual raies of hir eies as he, I saie, outstrippeth the nimblest trippers of his feathered condition in footman-shippe, onely spurd on with the needle quickning goade vnder his side, so hee no lesse burning sighted than the Estrich, spurd on to the race of honor by the sweete raies of his mistres eies, perswaded himselfe hee should outstrip all other in running to the goale of glorie only animated and incited by her excellence. And as the Estrich wil eat iron, swallow anie hard mettall whatsoeuer, so would he refuse no iron aduenture, no hard taske whatsoeuer, to sit in the grace of so fayre a commander. The order of his shield was this, it was framed like a burning glasse, beset round with flame colour feathers, on the outside whereof was his mistres picture adorned as beautifull as art could portrature, on the inside a naked sword tied in a true loue knot, the mot, *Militat omtiis amans*. Signifieng that in a true loue knot his sword was tide to defend and maintaine the high features of his mistres.

Next him entered the blacke knight, whose beauer was pointed all torne & bloudie, as though he had new come from combatting with a Beare, his head piece seemed to bee a little ouen fraught full with smoothering flames, for nothing but sulphure and smoake voided out at the cleftes of his beauer. His bases were all imbrodered with snakes & adders, ingendred of the abundance of innocent bloud that was shed. His horses trappinges were throughout bespangled with hunnie spottes, which are no blemishes, but ornaments. On his shield he bare the Sunne full shining on a diall at his going downe, the word *sufficit tandem*.

After him followed the knight of the Owle, whose armor was a stubd tree ouergrowen with iuie, his helmet fashioned lyke an owle sitting on the top of this iuie, on his bases were wrought all kinde of birdes as on the grounde wondering about him, the word, *Ideo mirum quia monstrunty* his horses furniture was framed like a cart, scattering whole sheaues of corne amongst hogs, the word *Liberalitas liberalitate perit*. On his shield a bee intangled in sheepes wooll, the mot *Frontis nulla fides*. The fourth that succeeded was a well proportioned knight in an armor imitating rust, whose head piece was prefigured like flowers growing in a narrowe pot, where they had not anie space to spread their roots or dispearse their florishing. His bases embelisht with open armed handes scattering golde amongst tranchions, the word *Cura futuri est*. His horse was harnished with leaden chaines, hauing the outside guilt, or at least saffrond in stead of guilt, to decypher a holie or golden pretence of a couetous purpose, the sentence *Cani capilli mei compedes*, on his target he had a number of crawling wormes kept vnder by a blocke, the faburthen, *Speramus lucent*. The fift was the forsaken knight, whose helmet was crowned with nothing but cipresse and willow garlands, ouer his armor he had on *I limons* nuptiall robe died in a duskie yelow, and all to be defaced and discoloured with spots & staines. The enigma, *Nosquoque floritnus*, as who shuld saie, we haue bin in fashion, his stead was adorned with orenge tawnie eies, such as those haue that haue the yellowe iandies, that make all things yellow they looke vpon, with this briefe, *Qui inuident egent*. Those that enuie are hungrie. The sixth was the knight of the stormes, whose helmet was round moulded like the Moone, and all his armour like waues, whereon the shine of the Moone sleightly siluerd, perfectly represented Mooneshine in the water, his bases were the banks or shores that bounded in the streames. The spoke was this, *Frustra picus*, as much to say, as fruitles seruice. On his shield he set forth a lion driuen from his praie by a dunghill cocke. The worde, *Non vi sed voce*, not by violence but by his voice.

The seuenth had lyke the gyants that sought to scale heauen in despight of Jupiter, a mount ouerwhelming his head and whole bodie. His bases outlayde with armes and legges which the skirts of that mountain left vncouered. Under this did hee characterise a man desirous to climbe to the heauen of honour, kept vnder with the mountaine of his princes command, and yet had hee armes and legges exempted from the suppression of the mountaine. The word, *Tu mihi criminis author* (alluding to his Princes commaund) thou art the occasion of my imputed cowardise. His horse was trapt in the earthie stringes of tree rootes, which though their increase was stubbed downe to the grounde, yet were they not vtterly deaded, but hop'd for an after resurrection. The worde, *Spe alor*, I hope for a spring. Uppon his shield hee bare a ball striken downe with a mand that it might mount The worde, *Ferior vt efferar*, I suffer my selfe to bee contemned because I will climbe. The eighth had all his armour throughout engrayled lyke a crabbed brierie hawthorne bush, out of which notwithstanding sprung (as a good Childe of an ill Father) fragraunt Blossomes of delightfull Maye Flowers, that made (according to the nature of Maye) a most odoriferous smell. In middest of this his snowie curled top, rounde wrapped together, on the ascending of his creast sate a solitarie nightingale close encaged with a thorne at her breast, hauing this mot in her mouth, *Luctus monumenta manebunt*. At the foote of this bush represented on his bases, lay a number of blacke swolne Toades gasping for winde, and Summer liu'de grashoppers gaping after deaw, both which were choakt with excessiue drouth, and for want of shade. The word, *Nan sine vulnere viresco*, I spring not without impediments, alluding to the Toades and such lyke, that earst laye sucking at his rootes, but nowe were turnd out, and neere choakt with drought His horse was suited in blacke sandie earth (as adiacent to this bush) which was here and there patched with short burnt grasse, and as thicke inke dropped with toyling ants & emets as euer it might crall, who in the full of the summer moone, (ruddie garnished on his horses forehead) hoorded vp theyr prouision of grain agaynst winter. The word *Victrix fortuno sapientia*, prouidence preuents misfortune. On his shield he set forth the picture of death doing almes deeds to a number of poore desolate children. The word, *Nemo alius explicate* No other man takes pittie vpon vs. What his meaning was heerein I cannot imagine, except death had done him and his brethren some greate good turne in ridding them of some vntoward parent or kinsman that woulde haue beene their confusion, for else I cannot see howe death shoulde haue beene sayde to doe almes deedes, except he had depriued them sodainly of their liues, to deliuer them out of some further miserie, which coulde not in anie wise bee because they were yet liuing.

The ninth was the infant knight, who on his armour had ennameld a poore young infant, put into a shippe without tackling, masts, furniture, or any thing. This weather beaten and ill apparelled shippe was shaddowed on his bases, and the slender compasse of his body set forth the right picture of an infant The waues wherein the ship was tossed were fretted on his steads trappings so mouingly, that euer as he offered to bounde or stirre, they seemed to bounse, and tosse, and sparkle brine out of theyr hoarie siluer billowes. Theyr mot, *Inopem me copia fecit*, as much to saie, as the rich praye makes the theefe.

On his shielde hee expressed an olde Goate that made a young tree to wither onely with biting it. The worde thereto *Primo extinguor in ouo*, I am frostbitten ere I come out of the blade.

It were here too tedious to manifest all the discontented or amorous deuises yt were vsed in that turnament. The shieldes onely of some few I wil touch to make short worke. One bare for his impresse the eies of yong swallowes comming againe after they were pluckt out, with this mot, *Et addit et addimit*, your beautie both bereaues and restores my sight. Another a siren smiling when the sea rageth and ships are ouerwhelmed, including a cruell woman, that laughs, singes and scornes at her louers tears, and the tempests of his despaire, the word *Cuncta pereunt*, all my labor is ill imploid. A third being troubled with a curst, a trecherous and wanton wanton wife, vsed this similitude. On his shild he caused to be limmed *Pompeies* ordinance for paracides, as namely a man put into a sack with a cocke, a serpent and an ape, interpreting that his wife was a cocke for her crowing, a serpent for her stinging, and an ape for her vnconstant wantonnesse, with which ill qualities hee was so beset, that thereby hee was throwen into a sea of grief. The worde *Extremum malorum mulier*, The vtmost of euils is a woman. A fourth, who being a person of suspected religion, was continually hanted with intelligencers and spies that thought to praie vppon him for that hee had, he could not deuise which waie to shape them off, but by making away that he had. To obscure this, hee vsed no other fansie but a number of blinde flies, whose eies the colde had closed, the word *Aurum reddit acutissimum*, Gold is the onely phisicke for the eiesight A fifth, whose mistres was fallen into a consumption, and yet would condiscend to no treatie of loue, emblazond for his complaint, grapes that witherd for want of pressing. The dittie to the mot, *Quid regna sine vsu*. I will rehearse no more, but I haue an hundred other, let this be the vpshot of these shewes, they were the admirablest that euer Florence yelded. To particularize their maner of encounter, were to describe the whol art of tilting. Some had like to haue falle ouer their horse neck and so breake their neckes in breaking their staues. Others ranne at a buckle in stead of a button, & peraduenture whetted their spears pointes, idlely gliding on their enemies sides, but did no other harme. Others ranne a crosse at theyr aduersaries left elbow, yea, and by your leaue sometimes let not the lists scape scot-free they were so eager. Others because they would be sure not to be vnsadled with the shocke, when they came to the speares vtmost proofe, they threw it ouer the right shoulder, and so tilted backward, for forwarde they durst not Another had a monstrous spite at the pommell of his riuals saddle, and thought to haue thrust his speare twixt his legges without rasing anie skinne, and carried him cleane awaie on it as a coolestaffe. Another held his speare to his nose, or his nose to his speare, as though he had ben discharging a caliuer, and ranne at the right foote of his fellowes stead. Onely the earle of Surry my master obserued y true measures of honor, and made all his encounterers new scoure their armor in the dust. So great was his glorie y daie, as *Geraldine* was therby eternally glorifide. Neuersuch a bountifull master came amongst the heralds (not that he did inrich the with anie plentifull purse largesse) but that by his sterne assaultes hee tithed them more rich offals of bases, of helmets, of armour, than the rent of their offices came to in ten yeres before. What would you haue more, the trumpets proclaimed him master of the field, the trumpets proclaimed *Geraldine* the exceptionlesse fayrest of women. Euerie one striued to magnifie him more than other. The Duke of Florence, whose name (as my memorie serueth me) was *Paschal de Medices*, offered him such large proffers to staie with him as it were vncredible to report He would not, his desire was as hee had done in Florence, so to proceede throughout all the chiefe cities in Italy. If you aske why he began not this at Venice first. It was because he would let Florence his mistres natiue citie haue the maidenhead of his chiualrie. As hee came backe againe hee thought to haue enacted something there worthie the Annals of posteritie, but he was debard both of that and all his other determinations, for continuing in feasting and banketting with the Duke of Florence and the Princes of Italy there assembled, posthast letters came to him from the king his master, to returne as speedily as he could possible into England, wherby his fame was quite cut off by the shins, and there was no repriue but *Bazelus manus*, hee must into England, and I with my curtizan trauelled forward in Italy.

What aduentures happened him after we parted, I am ignorant, but Florence we both forsooke, and I hauing a wonderful ardent inclination to see Rome the Queen of the world, & metropolitane mistres of all other cities, made thether with my bag and baggage as fast as I could.

Attained thether, I was lodged at the house of one *Iohannes de Imola* a Roman caualiero. Who being acquainted with my curtisans deceased doting husband, for his sake vsd vs with all the familiaritie that might be. He shewed vs all the monuments that were to be seene, which are as many as ther haue beene Emperours, Consuls, Orators, Conquerours, famous painters or plaiers in Rome. Till this daie not a Romane (if he be a right Romane in deed) will kill a rat, but he will haue some registred remembrance of it There was a poore fellowe during my remainder ther, that for a new trick he had inuented of killing *Cymess* & scorpions, had his mountebank banner hung vp on a high piller, with an inscription about it longer than the king of Spaines stile. I thought these *Cymesses* like the Cimbrians had bene some strange nation hee had brought vnder, & they were no more but things like sheepelice, which aliue haue the venomost sting that may be, and being dead do stinke out of measure. Saint Austen compareth heretiques vnto them. The chiefest thing that my eyes delighted in, was the church of the 7. Sibels, which is a most miraculous thing. All their prophesies and oracles being there enroulde, as also the beginning and ending of their whole catalogue of the heathen Gods, with their manner of worship. There are a number of other shrines and statues also dedicated to their Emperors, and withal some statues of idolatrie reserued for detestation. I was at *Pontius Pilates* house and pist against it There is the prison yet packt vp together (an old rotten thing) where the man that was condemned to death, and could haue no bodie come to him and succour him but was searcht, was kept aliue a long space by sucking his daughters breasts.

These are but the shop dust of the sights that I saw, and in truth I dyd not beholde with anie care hereafter to report, but contented my eie for the present, and so let them passe. Should I memorize halfe the myracles which they there tolde me had beene done about martyres tombes, or the operations of the earth of the sepulchre, and other reliques brought from Jerusalem, I should bee counted the monstrous Her that euer came in print.

The mines of *Pompeies* theater, reputed one of the nine wonders of the worlde, *Gregory* the sixths Tombe, *Priscillas* Grate, or the thousands of Piliers arreared amongst the raced foundations of old *Rome*, it were heere friuolous to specifie: since he that hath but once drunke with a traueller talkes of them. Let mee bee a Historiographer of my owne misfortunes, and not meddle with the continued Trophees of so olde a triumphing Citie.

At my first comming to *Rome*, I being a youth of the English cut, ware my haire long, went apparailed in light coulours, and imitated foure or fiue sundrie Nations in my attyre at once: which no sooner was noated, but I had all the boyes of the Citie in a swarme wondering about mee. I had not gone a little farther, but certaine Officers crost the waie of me, and demanded to see my rapier: which when they found (as also my dagger) with his poynt vnblunted, they would haue hal'd me headlong to the Strappado, but that with money

I appeased them: and my fault was more pardonable in that I was a stranger, altogether ignorant of their customes.

Note by the waye, that it is the vse in *Rome*, for all men whatsoeuer to weafe their haire short: which they doo not so much for conscience sake, or anie religion they place in it, but because the extremitie of the heate is such there, that if they should not doo so, they should not haue a haire left on their heads to stand vpright, when they were scard with sprights. And hee is counted no Gentleman amongst them that goes not in black: they dresse their iesters and fooles onely in fresh colours, and say variable garments doo argue vnstayednes and vnconstancie of affections.

The reason of their straight ordinaunce of carrying weapons without points is this. The *Bandettos* which are certaine outlawes that lye betwixt *Rome & Naples*, and besiege the passage that none can trauell that way without robbing: Now and then hired for some few crownes, they wil steale to Rome and doe a murther, and betake them to their heeles againe. Disguised as they go, they are not knowen from strangers, sometimes they will shroude themselues vnder the habite of graue citizens. In this consideration neither citizen nor stranger, gentleman, knight, marques, or any may weare anie weapon endamageable vppon paine of the strappado. I bought it out, let others buy experience of me better cheape.

To tell you of the rare pleasures of their gardens, theyr baths, their vineyards, their galleries, were to write a second part of the gorgeous Gallerie of gallant deuices. Why, you should not come into anie mans house of account, but hee had fishponds and litle orchards on the top of his leads. If by rain or anie other meanes those ponds were so full they need to bee fluste or let out, euen of their superfluities they made melodious vse, for they had great winde instruments in stead of leaden spoutes, that went duely in consort, onely with this waters rumbling discent I saw a summer banketting house belonging to a marchant, that was the meruaile of the worlde, & could not be matcht except God should make another paradise. It was builte rounde of greene marble, like a Theater without, within there was a heauen and earth comprehended both vnder one roofe, the heauen was a cleere ouerhanging vault of christall, wherein the Sunne and Moone, and each visible Starre had his true similitude, shine, scituation, and motion, and by what enwrapped arte I cannot conceiue, these spheares in their proper orbes obserued their circular wheelings and turnings, making a certaine kinde of soft angelical murmering musicke in their often windings & going about, which musick the philosophers say in the true heauen by reason of the grosenes of our senses we are not capable of. For the earth it was counterfeited in that likenes that Adam lorded out it before his fall. A wide vast spacious roome it was, such as we would conceit prince Arthurs hall to be, where he feasted all his knightes of the round table together euerie penticost The floore was painted with y beautifullest floures that euer mans eie admired, which so lineally wer delineated, that he that viewd them a farre off, and had not directly stood poaringly ouer them, would haue sworne they had liued in deede. The wals round about were hedgde with Oliues and palme trees, and all other odoriferous fruit-bearing plants, which at anie solemne intertainment dropt mirrhe and frankensence. Other trees y bare no fruit, were set in iust order one against another, and diuided the roome into a number of shadie lanes, leauing but one ouer-spreading pine tree arbour, where wee sate and banketted. On the well clothed boughes of this conspiracie of pine trees against the resembled Sunne beames, were pearcht as many sortes of shrill breasted birdes, as the Summer hath allowed for singing men in her siluane chappels. Who though there were bodies without soules, & sweete resembled substances without sense, yet by the mathematicall experimentes of long siluer pipes secretly inrinded in the intrailes of the boughs whereon they sate, and vndiscerneablie conuaid vnder their bellies into their small throats sloaping, they whistled and freely carold theyr naturall field note. Neyther went those siluer pipes straight, but by many edged vnsundred writhings, & crankled wandrings aside strayed from bough to bough into an hundred throates. But into this siluer pipe so writhed and wandering aside, if anie demand how the wind was breathed. Forsoth ye tail of the siluer pipe stretcht it selfe into the mouth of a great paire of bellowes, where it was close soldered, and bailde about with yron, it coulde not stirre or haue anie vent betwixt. Those bellowes with the rising and falling of leaden plummets wounde vp on a wheele, dyd beate vp and downe vncessantly, and so gathered in wind, seruing with one blast all the snarled pipes to and fro of one tree at once. But so closely were all those organizing implements obscured in the corpulent trunks of the trees, that euerie man there present renounst coniectures of art, and sayd it was done by inchantment.

One tree for his fruit bare nothing but inchained chiriping birdes, whose throates beeing conduit pipt with squared narrow shels, & charged siring-wise with searching sweet water, driuen in by a little wheele for the nonce, and fed it afarre of, made a spirting sound, such as chirping is, in bubling vpwards through the rough crannies of their closed bils.

Under tuition of the shade of euerie tree that I haue signified to be in this round hedge, on delightfull leauie cloysters, lay a wylde tyrannous beast asleepe all prostrate: vnder some two together, as the Dogge nusling his nose vnder the necks of the Deare, the Wolfe glad to let the Lambe lye vpon hym to keepe him warme, the Lyon suffering the Asse to cast hys legge ouer him: preferring one honest vnmannerly frend, before a number of croutching picke-thankes. No poysonous beast there reposed, (poyson was not before our parent *Adam* transgressed). There were no sweete-breathing Panthers, that would hyde their terrifying heads to betraye: no men imitating *Hyonaes*. that chaunged their sexe to seeke after bloud. Wolues as now when they are hungrie eate earth, so then did they feede on earth onely, and abstained from innocent flesh. The Unicorne did not put his home into the streame to chase away venome before he drunke, for there was no such thing as venome extant in the water or on the earth. Serpents were as harmlesse to mankinde, as they are still one to another: the rose had no cankers, the leaues no caterpillers, the sea no *Syrens*, the earth no vsurers. Goates then bare wooll, as it is recorded in *Sicily* they doo yet. The torride Zone was habitable; onely Jayes loued to steale gold and siluer to build their nests withall, and none cared for couetous clientrie, or running to the Indies. As the Elephant vnderstands his countrey speach, so euerie beast vnderstood what men spoke. The ant did not hoord vp against winter, for there was no winter but a perpetuall spring, as *Ouid* sayth. No frosts to make the greene almond tree counted rash and improuident, in budding soonest of all other. or the mulberie tree a strange polititian, in blooming late and ripening early. The peach tree at the first planting was frutefull and wholesome, wheras now til it be transplanted, it is poysonous and hatefull. Yong plants for their sap had balme, for their yeolow gumme glistering amber. The euening deawd not water on flowers, but honnie. Such a golden age, such a good age, such an honest age was set foorth in this banquetting house.

O *Rome*, if thou hast in thee such soule-exalting obiects: what a thing is heauen in comparison of thee, of which *Mercators* globe is a perfecter modell than thou art? Yet this I must say to the shame of vs Protestants, if good workes may merit heauen, they doo them, we talke of them. Whether superstition or no makes the vnprofitable seruants, that let pulpets decide: but there, you shall haue the brauest Ladies in gownes of beaten gold, washing pilgrimes and poore souldiours feete and dooing nothing they and their wayting mayds all the yeare long, but making shirts and bandes for them against they come by in distresse. Their hospitalls are more like noblemens houses than otherwise: so richly furnished, cleane kept, and hot perfumed, that a souldiour would thinke it a sufficient recompence for his trauell and his wounds, to haue such a heauenly retyring place. For the Pope and his pontificalibus I will not deale with, onely I will dilate vnto you what hapned whiles I was in *Rome*.

So it fell out, that it being a vehement hot summer when I was a soiourner there, there entred such a hotspurd plague as hath not been heard of: why it was but a word and a blow, Lord haue mercie vpon vs, and he was gone. Within three quarters of a yere in that one citie there dyed of it a hundred thousand: Looke in *Lanquets* Chronicle and you shall finde it. To smell of a nosegay, that was poysond: and turne your nose to a house, that had the plague, it was all one. The clouds like a number of cormorants, that keepe their corne till it stinke and is mustie, kept in their stinking exhalations, till they had almost stifled all *Romes* inhabitants. Phisitions, greedines of golde made them greedie of their destinie. They would come to visite those, with whose infirmities their arte had no affinitie: and euen as a man with a fee should bee hyred to hang himselfe, so would they quietly goe home and dye presently after they had been with their patients. All day and all night long carremen did nothing but goe vp and downe the streetes with their carts and crye, Haue you anie dead to burie, haue you anie dead to burie: and had manie times out of one house their whole loading: one graue was the sepulcher of seuenscore, one bed was the altar whereon whole families were offered.

The wals were hoard and furd with the moist scorching steam of their desolation. Euen as before a gun is shot off, a stinking smoake funnels out, and prepares the waie for him, so before anie gaue vp the ghost, death araied in a stinking smoke stopt his nostrils, and cramd it selfe full into his mouth, that closed vp his fellowes eyes, to giue him warning to prepare for his funeral. Some dide sitting at their meate, others as they were asking counsell of the phisition for their friendes. I saw at the house where I was hosted, a maide bring her master warme broth for to comfort him, and she sinke downe dead her self ere he had halfe eate it vp.

During this time of visitation, there was a Spaniard, one *Esdras* of Granado, a notable Bandetto, authorized by ye pope, because he assisted him in some murthers. This villain colleagued with one *Bartol* a desperate Italian, practised to breake into those rich mens houses in the night where the plague had most rained, and if there were none but the mistres and maid left aliue, to rauish them both, and bring awaie all the wealth they could fasten on. In a hundred chief citizens houses where the hand of God had bin, they put this outrage in vse. Thogh the women so rauished cride out, none durst come nere them, for feare of catching their deaths by them, & some thought they cried out onely with the tyrannie of the maladie. Amongst the rest the house where I lay he inuaded, where all being snatcht vp by the sicknesse but the good wife of the house, a noble and chast matrone called *Heraclide* and her *Zanie*, and I & my curtizan, he knocking at the dore late in the night, ranne in to the matrone, & left me and my loue to the mercie of his companion. Who finding me in bed (as the time requird) ranne at me full with his rapier, thinking I would resist him, but as good lucke was I escapt him & betooke me to my pistoll in the window vncharged. He fearing it had bene charged, threatned to run her through if I once offered but to aime at him, Foorth ye chamber he dragd her, holding his rapier at hir hart, whilest I stil crid out, Saue her, kil me, & Ile ransome her with a thousand duckets: but lust preuailed, no praiers would be heard. Into my chamber I was lockt, and watchmen charged (as he made semblance when there was none there) to knocke me downe with their halberdes, if I stirde but a foote downe the staires. So threw I my selfe pensiue againe on my pallat, and dard all the deuils in hell now I was alone to come and fight with me one after another in defence of that detestable rape. I beat my head against the wals and cald them bauds, because they wold see such a wrong committed, and not fall vpon him. To returne to *Heraclide* below, whom the vgliest of all bloud suckers *Esdras of Granado* had vnder shrift. First he assayled her with rough meanes, and slew her *Zanie* at her foote, that stept before her in rescue. Then when al armed resist was put to flight, he assaied her with honie speech, & promised her more iewells and giftes than hee was able to pilfer in an hundred yeres after. He discourst vnto her how he was countenanced and borne out by the pope, and how many execrable murthers with impunitie he had executed on them that displeasde him. This is the eight score house (quoth he) that hath done homage vnto me, and here I will preuaile, or I will bee torne in pieces. Ah quoth *Heraclide* (with a hart renting sigh) art thou ordaind to be a worse plague to me than ye plague it selfe? Haue I escapt the hands of God to fal into the hands of man? Heare me *Iehouah*, & be merciful in ending my miserie. Dispatch me incontinent dissolute homicide deaths vsurper. Here lies my husband stone colde on the dewie floore. If thou beest of more power than God, to strike me speedily, strike home, strike deep, send me to heauen with my husband. Aie me, it is the spoyl of my honor thou seekest in my soules troubled departure, thou art some deuill sent to tempt me. Auoide from me sathan, my soule is my sauiours, to him I haue bequeathed it, from him can no man take it. Jesu, Jesu spare mee vndefiled for thy spouse, Jesu, Jesu neuer faile those that put their trust in thee. With that she fell in a sowne, and her eies in their closing seemed to spaune forth in their outward sharpe corners new created seed pearle, which the world before neuer set eie on. Soone he rigorously reuiued her, & tolde her yt he had a charter aboue scripture, she must yeld, she should yeld, see who durst remoue her out of his hands. Twixt life and death thus she faintly replied. How thinkest thou, is there a power aboue thy power, if there be, he is here present in punishment, and on thee will take present punishment if thou persistest in thy enterprise. In the tyme of securitie euerie man sinneth, but when death substitutes one frend his special bayly to arrest another by infection, and dispearseth his quiuer into ten thousand hands at once, who is it but lookes about him? A man that hath an vneuitable huge stone hanging only by a haire ouer his head, which he lookes euerie Pater noster while to fall and pash him in pecces, will not he be submissiuely sorrowfull for his transgressions, refraine himselfe from the least thought of folly, and purifie his spirit with contrition and penitence? Gods hand like a huge stone hangs vneuitably ouer thy head: what is the plague, but death playing the prouost marshall, to execute all those that wil not be called home by anie other meanes. This my deare knights body is a quiuer of his arrowes, which alreadie are shot into thee inuisible. Euen as the age of goates is knowen by the knots on their homes, so think the anger of God apparently visioned or showne vnto thee in the knitting of my browes. A hundred haue I buried out of my house, at all whose departures I haue been present: a hundreds infection is mixed with my breath, loe, now I breath vpon thee, a hundred deaths come vpon thee. Repent betimes, imagine there is a hell though not a heauen: that hell thy conscience is throughly acquainted with, if thou hast murdred halfe so manie, as thou vnblushingly braggest. As *Mocenas* in the latter end of his dayes was seuen yeres without sleepe, so these seuen weekes haue I took no slumber, my eyes haue kept continuall watch against the diuell my enemie: death I deemed my frend (frends flie from vs in aduersitie), death, the diuell & al the ministring spirits of temptation are watching about thee to intrap thy soule by my abuse to eternall damnation. It is thy soule only thou maist saue by sauing mine honor.

Death will haue thy bodie infallibly for breaking into my house, that he had selected for his priuate habitation. If thou euer camst of a woman, or hop'st to be sau'd by the seed of a woman, spare a woman. Deares oppressed with dogs, when they cannot take soyle, runne to men for succor: to whom should women in their disconsolate and desperate estate run, but to men like the Deare for succour and sanctuarie. If thou bee a man thou wilt succour me, but if thou be a dog & a brute beast, thou wilt spoile me, defile me & teare me. either renounce Gods image, or renounce the wicked minde that thou bearest.

These words might haue moou'd a compound hart of yron and adamant, but in his hart they obtained no impression: for he sitting in his chaire of state against the doore all the while that she pleaded, leaning his ouerhanging gloomie eybrowes on the pommell of his vnsheathed sword, hee neuer lookt vp or gaue her a word: but when he perceiued shee expected his answere of grace or vtter perdition, he start vp and took her currishly by the neck, and askt her how long he should stay for her Ladiship.

Thoutelst me (quoth he) of the plague, and the heauie hand of God, and thy hundred infected breaths in one: I tel thee I haue cast the dice an hundred times for the galleyes in *Spaine*, and yet still mist the ill chance. Our order of casting is this, If there be a generall or captaine new come home from the warres, & hath some foure or fiue hundred crownes ouerplus of the kings in his hand, & his souldiors al paid, he makes proclamation, that whatsoeuer two resolute men will goe to dice for it, and win the bridle or lose the saddle, to such a place let them repaire, and it shall be ready for them. Thither go I & finde another such needie squire resident. The dice runne, I win, he is vndone. I winning haue the crownes, he loosing is carried to the galleys. This is our custome, which a hundred times and more hath paid mee custome of crownes, when the poore fellowes haue gone to *Gehenna*, had course bread and whipping chere all their life after. Now thinkest thou that I who so oft haue escapd such a number of hellish dangers, only depending on the turning of a few pricks, can be scarebugd with the plague? what plague canst thou name worse than I haue had? whether diseases, imprisonment, pouertie, banishment, I haue past through them all. My owne mother gaue I a box of the eare to, and brake her neck down a pair of stairs, because she would not go in to a gentleman, when I bad her: my sister I solde to an olde Leno, to make his best of her: anie kinswoman that I haue, knew I shee were not a whore, my selfe would make her one: thou art a whore, thou shalt bee a whore in spite of religion or precise ceremonies.

Therewith he flew vpon her, and threatned her with his sword, but it was not that he meant to wounde her with. Hee graspt her by the iuorie throate, and shooke her as a mastiffe would shake a yong beare, swearing & flaring he would teare out her wesand if she refused. Not content with that sauage constraint, he slipt his sacriligious hand from her lilly lawne skinned necke, and inscarfte it in her long siluer lockes, which with strugling were vnrould. Backward hee dragd her, euen as a man backward would plucke a tree downe by the twigs, and then like a traitor that is drawen to execution on a hurdle, he traileth her vp and downe the chamber by those tender vntwisted braids, and setting his barbarous foote on her bare snowie breast, bad her yeeld or haue her wind stampt out She crid, stamp, stifle me in my hair, hang me vp by it on a beame, and so let mee die rather than I shoulde go to heauen wyth a beame in my eie. No (quoth he) nor stampt, nor stifled, nor hanged, nor to heauen shalt thou go til I haue had my wil of thee, thy busie armes in these silken fetters Ile infold. Dismissing her haire from his fingers, and pinnioning her elbowes therwithal, she strugled, she wrested, but al was in vain. So strugling & so resisting, her iewels did sweate, signifieng there was poison comming towards her. On the hard boords hee threw her, and vsed his knee as an yron ram to beate ope the two leaude gate of her chastitie. Her husbands dead bodie he made a pillow to his abhomination. Coniecture the rest, my words sticke fast in the mire and are cleane tyred, would I had neuer vndertooke this tragicall tale. Whatsoeuer is borne to haue end. Thus endeth my tale, his boorish lust was glutted, his beastly desire satisfied, what in the house of any worth was carriageable, he put vp and went his way.

Let not your sorow die, you that haue read the proeme and narration of this elegiacal history. Shew you haue quick wits in sharpe conceit of compassion. A woman that hath viewd all her children sacrificed before her eies, & after the first was slaine wipt the sword with her apron to prepare it for the clenly murther of the second, and so on forwarde till came to the empiercing of the seuenteenth of her loines, will you not giue her great allowance of anguish. This woman, this matrone, this forsaken *Heraclide*, hauing buried fourteene children in fiue dayes, whose eyes she howlingly closed, and caught many wrinckles with funerall kisses: besides, hauing her husband within a day after layd forth as a comfortlesse corse, a carrionly blocke, that could neither eate with her, speak with her, nor weepe with her, is she not to be borne withall though her bodie swells wyth a tympanie of teares, though her speach be as impatient as vnhappy *Hecubaes*, though her head raues and her braine doates? Deuise with your selues that you see a corse rising from his heirce after hee is carried to Church, and such another suppose *Heraclide* to bee, rising from the couch of enforced adulterie.

Her eyes were dimme, her cheekes bloudlesse, her breath smelt earthie, her countenance was ghastly. Up she rose after she was deflowred, but loath she arose, as a reprobate soule rising to the day of iudgement. Looking on the tone side as she rose, she spide her husbands bodie lying vnder her head: Ah then she bewayled as *Cephaius* when hee had kild *Procris* vnwittingly, or *Oedipus* when ignorant he had slaine his owne father, and knowen his mother incestuously. This was her subdued reasons discourse.

Haue I liu'd to make my husbands bodie the beere to carry me to hell, had filthie pleasure no other pillowe to leane vpon but his spreaded limmes? On thy flesh my fault shall bee imprinted at the day of resurrection. O beauty, the bait ordained to insnare the irreligious: rich men are robd for theyr welth, women are dishonested for being too faire. No blessing is beautie but a curse: curst bee the time that euer I was begotten: curst be the time that my mother brought me forth to tempt. The serpent in paradice did no more, the serpent in paradice is damned sempiternally: why should not I hold my selfe damned (if predestinations opinions be true) that am predestinate to this horrible abuse. The hogge dieth presently if he loseth an eye: with the hogge haue I wallowed in the myre, I haue lost my eye of honestie, it is cleane pluckt out with a strong hand of vnchastitie: what remaineth but I dye? Die I will, though life be vnwilling: no recompence is there for mee to redeeme my compelled offence, but with a rigorous compelled death. Husband, He be thy wife in heauen: let not thy pure deceasing spirite despise me when we meete, because I am tyrannously polluted. The diuell, the belier of our frayltie, and common accuser of mankinde, cannot accuse me though he would of vnconstrained submitting. If anie guilt be mine, this is my fault, that I did not deforme my face, ere it shuld so impiously allure. Hauing passioned thus a while, she hastely ranne and lookt her selfe in her glasse to see if her sinne were not written on her forhead: with looking shee blusht though none lookt vpon her but her owne reflected image.

Then began she againe. *Heu quam difficile est crimen non prodere vultu;* How hard is it not to bewray a mans fault by his forhead. My selfe doo but behold my selfe, and yet I blush: then God beholding me, shall not I bee ten times more ashamed? The Angells shall hisse at mee, the Saints and Martyrs flye from me: yea, God himselfe shall adde to the diuels damnation, because he suffred such a wicked creature to come before him. *Agamemnon* thou wert an infidell, yet when thou wentst to the Troian warre, thou leftst a Musitian at home with thy wife, who by playing the foote *Spondous* tyll thy returne, might keepe her in chastitie. My husband going to warre with the diuell and his enticements when hee surrendred, left no musition with me but mourning and melancholy: had he left anie, as *Aegistus* kild *Agamemnons* musition ere he could be succesfull, so surely would he haue been kild ere this *Aegistus* surceased. My distressed heart as the Hart when he looseth his homes is astonied, and sorrowfullie runneth to hide himselfe, so bee thou afflicted and distressed, hide thy selfe vnder the Almighties wings of mercie: sve, plead, intreate, grace is neuer denyed to them that aske. It may be denied, I may be a vessell ordained to dishonor. The onely repeale we haue from Gods vndefinite chastisement, is to chastise our selues in this world: and so I will, nought but death bee my pennance, gracious and acceptable may it bee: my hand and my knife shall manumit me out of the horror of minde I endure. Farewell life that hast lent me nothing but sorrow: farewell sinne sowed flesh, that hast more weeds than flowers, more woes than ioyes.

Point pierce, edge enwyden, I patiently affoord thee a sheath: spurre foorth my soule to mount poast to heauen. Iesu forgiue me, Iesu receiue me.

So throughly stabd fell she downe, and knockt her head against her husbands bodie: wherewith, hee not hauing beene ayred his full foure and twentie houres, start as out of a dreame: whiles I through a crannie of my vpper chamber vnseeled, had beheld all this sad spectacle. Awaking, hee rubd his head too and fro, and wyping his eyes with his hand began to looke about him. Feeling some thing lye heauie on his breast, he turnd it off, and getting vpon his legges lighted a candle.

Heere beginneth my purgatorie. For he good man comming into the hall with the candle, and spying his wife wyth her haire about her eares defiled and massacred, and his simple *Zanie Capestrano* run thorough, tooke a halberde in hys hand, and running from chamber to chamber to search who in his house was likely to doo it, at length found me lying on my bed, the doore lockt to me on the outside, and my rapier vnsheathed on the windowe: wherewith hee straight coniectured it was I. And calling the neighbours harde by, sayd I had caused my selfe to bee lockt into my chamber after that sort, sent awaye my curtizane whome I called my wife, and made cleane my rapier, because I would not bee suspected. Uppon this was I laide in prison, should haue been hanged, was brought to the ladder, had made a ballet for my farewell in a readines called *Wiltons wantonnes,* and yet for all that scap'd dancing in a hempen circle. He that hath gone through manie perils and returned safe from them, makes but a merriment to dilate them. I had the knot vnder my eare, there was faire playe, the hangman had one halter, and another about my necke, which was fastned to the gallowes, the riding deuice was almost thrust home, and his foote on my shoulder to presse me downe, when I made my saint-like confession as you haue heard before, that such & such men at such an houre brake into the house, slew the Zanie, tooke my curtizan, lockt me into my chamber, rauisht *Heraclide,* and finally how shee slew her selfe.

Present at the execution was there a banisht English Earle, who hearing that a countreyman of his was to suffer for such a notable murder, came to heare his confession, and see if hee knew him. He had not heard me tell halfe of that I haue recited, but hee craued audience, and desired the execution might be staid.

Not two dayes since it is Gentlemen and noble *Romanes* (said he) since going to be let bloud in a barbars shop agaynst the infection, all on a suddaine in a great tumult and vproare was there brought in one *Bartoll* an Italian greeuously wounded and bloudie. I seeming to commiserate his harmes, courteously questiond him with what ill debters he had met, or how or by what casualtie he came to be so arraid. O quoth he long I haue liu'd sworne brothers in sensualitie with one *Esdras of Granado,* fiue hundred rapes and murders haue wee committed betwixt vs. When our iniquities were growen to the height, and God had determined to counterchecke our amitie, wee came to the house of *Iohannes de Imola* (whom this yong gentleman hath named) there did he iustifie al those rapes in manner and forme as the prisoner here hath confest. But loe an accident after, which neither he nor this audience is priuie too. *Esdras of Granado* not content to haue rauisht the matrone *Heraclide* and robd her, after he had betooke hym from thence to his heeles, light on his companion *Bartol* with his curtizan: whose pleasing face hee had scarce winkingly glaunc'd on, but hee pickt a quarrell with *Bartoll* to haue her from him. On this quarrell they fought *Bartoll* was wounded to the death, *Esdras* fled, and the faire dame left to go whither she would. This *Bartoll* in the barbars shoppe freely acknowledged, as both the barbar and his man, and other heere present can amply depose. Deposed they were, their oathes went for currant, I was quit by proclamation, to the banisht Earle I came to render thankes: when thus he examind me and schoold me.

Countriman, tell mee what is the occasion of thy straying so farre out of *England* to visit this strange Nation. If it bee languages, thou maist learne them at home, nought but lasciuiousnes is to be learned here. Perhaps to be better accounted of than other of thy condition, thou ambitiously vndertakest this voyage: these insolent fancies are but *Icarus* fethers, whose wanton wax melted against the sunne, will betray thee into a sea of confusion. The first traueller was *Cayn*, and hee was called a vagabond runnagate on the face of the earth. Trauaile like the trauaile wherein smithes put wilde horses when they shoo them, is good for nothing but to tame and bring men vnder. God had no greater curse to lay vppon the *Israelites*, than by leading them out of their owne countrey to liue as slaues in a strange land. That which was their curse, we Englishmen count our chief blessednes; he is no body that hath not traueld: wee had rather liue as slaues in another land, croutch and cap, and bee seruile to euerie iealous Italians and proude Spaniards humor, where wee may neyther speake looke nor doo anie thing, but what pleaseth them, than liue as freemen and Lords in our owne countrey. He that is a traueller must haue the backe of an asse to beare all, a tung like the tayle of a dog to flatter all, the mouth of a hog to eate what is set before him, the eare of a merchant to heare all and say nothing: and if this be not the highest step of thraldome, there is no libertie or freedome. It is but a milde kind of subiection to be the seruant of one master at once, but when thou hast a thousand thousand masters, as the veriest botcher, tinker or cobler freeborne wil dominere ouer a forreiner, & think to bee his better or master in company: then shalt thou finde theres no such hell, as to leaue thy fathers house (thy natural habitation) to liue in the land of bondage. If thou doest but lend halfe a looke to a Romans or Italians wife, thy porredge shall bee prepared for thee, and cost thee nothing but thy life. Chance some of them break a bitter iest on thee, and thou retortst it seuerly, or seemest discontented: goe to thy chamber, & prouide a great banquet, for thou shalt bee sure to bee visited with guests in a maske the next night, when in kindnes and courtship thy throate shalbe cut, and the doers returne vndiscouered. Nothing so long of memorie as a dog, these Italians are old dogs, and will carrie an iniurie a whole age in memorie: I haue heard of a box on the eare that hath been reuenged thirtie yeare after. The Neopolitane carrieth the bloudiest wreakfull minde, and is the most secrete flearing murderer. Whereupon it is growne to a common prouerb, He giue him the Neapolitan shrug, when one meanes to play the villaine, and makes no boast of it.

The onely precept that a traueller hath most vse of, and shall finde most ease in, is that of *Epicharchus; Vigila & memor sis ne quid credos;* Beleeue nothing, trust no man: yet seeme thou as thou swallowedst all, suspectedst none, but wert easie to be gulled by euery one. *Multi fallere docuerunt* (as *Seneca* saith) *dum timent falli;* Many by showing their iealous suspect of deceit, haue made men seek more subtill meanes to deceiue them.

Alas, our Englishmen are the plainest dealing soules that euer God put life in: they are greedie of newes, and loue to be fed in their humors and heare themselues flattered the best that may be. Euen as *Philemon* a Comick Poet dyde with extreame laughter at the conceit of seeing an Asse eate fygges: so haue the Italians no such sport, as to see poore English asses how soberly they swallow Spanish figges deuour any hooke baited for them. He is not fit to trauell, that cannot with the Candians liue on serpents, make nourishing foode euen of poyson. Rats and mice engender by licking one another, he must licke, he must croutch, he must cogge, lye and prate, that either in the Court or a forraine Countrey will engender and come to preferment. Bee his feature what it will, if he be faire spoken he winneth frends: *Nonformosus erat, sed erat facundus Vlysses; Vlysses* the long traueller was not amiable, but eloquent. Some alleadge, they trauell to learne wit, but I am of this opinion, that as it is not possible for anie man to learne the Arte of Memorie, whereof *Tully, Quintillian, Seneca, and Hermannus Buschius* haue written so manie bookes, except he haue a naturall memorie before: so is it not possible for anie man to attaine anie great wit by trauell, except he haue the grounds of it rooted in him before. That wit which is thereby to be perfected or made stayd, is nothing but *Experientia longa malorum*, The experience of manie euills: the experience that such a man lost his life by this folly, another by that: such a young Gallant consumed his substance on such a Curtizan: these courses of reuenge a Merchant of *Venice* tooke against a Merchant of *Ferrara*: and this poynt of iustice was shewed by the Duke vppon the murtherer. What is heere but wee maye read in bookes and a great deale more too, without stirring our feete out of a warme studie.

Vobis alii ventorum prolia narrent, (saith Ouid) *Quasq; Scilla infestat, quasue Charybdis aquas*. Let others tell you wonders of the winde, How *Scalla* or *Charybdis* is enclinde.

—*vos quod quisque loquetur Credite*   —*Beleeue you what they say, but neuer trie*.

So let others tell you straunge accidents, treasons, poysonings, close packings in *Frounce, Spaine and Italy*: it is no harme for you to heare of them, but come not neere them. What is there in *Fraunce* to be learnd more than in *England*, but falshood in fellowship, perfect slouenrie, to loue no man but for my pleasure, to sweare *Ah par la mort Dieu* when a mans hammes are scabd. For the idle Traueller, (I meane not for the Souldiour) I haue knowen some that haue continued there by the space of halfe a dozen yeare, and when they come home, they haue hyd a little weerish leane face vnder a broad French hat, kept a terrible coyle with the dust in the streete in their long cloakes of gray paper, and spoke English strangely. Nought else haue they profited by their trauell, saue learnt to distinguish of the true *Burdeaux* Grape, and knowe a cup of neate *Gascoygne* wine, from wine of *Orleance* : yea and peraduenture this also, to esteeme of the poxe as a pimple, to weare a veluet patch on their face, and walke melancholy with their armes folded.

From *Spaine* what bringeth our Traueller? a scull cround hat of the fashion of an olde deepe poringer, a diminutiue Aldermans ruffe with shorte strings like the droppings of a mans nose, a close-bellied dublet comming downe with a peake behinde as farre as the crupper, and cut off before by the breast-boane like a partlet or neckercher, a wyde payre of gascoynes which vngatherd would make a couple of womens ryding kyrtles, huge hangers that haue halfe a Cowe hyde in them, a Rapyer that is lineally descended from halfe a dozen Dukes at the least. Let his cloake be as long or as short as you will: if long, it is fac'd with Turkey grogeran raueld; if short, it hath a cape like a calues tung, and is not so deep in his whole length, nor hath so much cloth in it I will iustifie, as onely the standing cape of a Dutchmans cloake. I haue not yet toucht all, for hee hath in eyther shoo as much taffaty for his tyings, as would serue for an ancient: which serueth him (if you will haue the mysterie of it) of the owne accord for a shoo-rag. A souldior and a braggart he is (thats concluded) he ietteth strouting, dancing on his toes with his hands vnder his sides. If you talke with him, hee makes a dish-cloath of his owne Countrey in comparison of *Spaine*; but if you vrge him more particularly wherein it exceeds, hee can giue no instance, but in *Spaine* they haue better bread than any we haue: when (poore hungry slaues) they may crumble it into water wel enough and make misons with it, for they haue not a good morsell of meate except it bee salt pilchers to eate with it al the yere long: and which is more, they are poore beggers, and lye in foule straw euery night.

Italy the paradice of the earth, and the Epicures heauen, how doth it forme our yong master? It makes him to kisse his hand like an ape, cringe his neck like a starueling, and play at hey passe repasse come aloft when hee salutes a man. From thence he brings the art of atheisme, the art of epicurising, the art of whoring, the art of poysoning, the art of Sodomitrie. The onely probable good thing they haue to keepe vs from vtterly condemning it, is, that it maketh a man an excellent Courtier, a curious carpet knight; which is by interpretation, a fine close leacher, a glorious hypocrite. It is now a priuie note amongst the better sort of men, when they would set a singular marke or brand on a notorious villaine, to say, he hath been in *Italy*.

With the Dane and the Dutchman I will not encounter, for they are simple honest men, that with *Danaus* daughters do nothing but fill bottomles tubs, & wil be drunk & snort in the midst of dinner: he hurts himselfe onely that goes thether, hee cannot lightly be damnd, for the vintners, the brewers, the malt-men and alewiues praye for him. Pitch and pay, they will play all day: score and borrow, they will wysh him much sorrowe. But lightly a man is nere the better for their praiers, for they commit al deadly sinne for the most part of them in mingling their drinke, the vintners in the highest degree.

Why iest I in such a necessary perswasiue discourse? I am a banisht exile from my countrie, though nere linkt in consanguinitie to the best: an Earle borne by birth, but a begger now as thou seest. These many yeres in *Italy* haue I liu'd an outlaw. A while I had a liberall pension of the Pope, but that lasted not, for he continued not: one succeeded him in his chaire, that car'd neither for Englishmen nor his owne countrimen. Then was I driu'n to picke vp my crums amongst the Cardinals, to implore the beneuolence & charitie of al the Dukes of Italy whereby I haue since made a poore shift to liue, but so liue, as I wish my selfe a thousand times dead.

Cum patriam amisi, tunc me periisse putato. When I was banisht, thinke I caught my bane.

The sea is the natiue soyle to fishes, take fishes from the sea, they take no ioy nor thriue, but perish straight. So likewise the birds remoued from the aire (the abode wherto they were borne) the beasts from the earth, and I from *England.* Can a lambe take delight to be suckled at the brests of a she-wolfe? I am a lambe nourisht with the milke of wolues, one that with the Ethiopians inhabiting ouer against *Meroe*, feede on nothing but scorpions: vse is another nature, yet ten times more contentiue, were nature restored to her kingdome from whence shee is excluded. Beleeue mee, no aire, no bread, no fire, no water agree with a man, or dooth him anye good out of his owne countrey. Colde frutes neuer prosper in a hot soile, nor hot in a cold. Let no man for any transitorie pleasure sell away the inheritance of breathing he hath in the place where he was born. Get thee home my yong lad, lay thy bones peaceably in the sepulcher of thy fathers, waxe old in ouerlooking thy grounds, bee at hand to close the eyes of thy kinred. The diuell and I am desperate, he of being restored to heauen, I of being recalled home.

Here he held his peace and wept. I glad of any opportunitie of a full poynt to part from him, told him I tooke his counsaile in worth, what laye in mee to requite in loue should not bee lacking. Some businesse that concerned mee highly cald mee away verie hastely, but another time I hop'd wee should meete. Verie hardly he let me goe, but I earnestly ouerpleading my occasions, at length he dismist mee, told mee where his lodging was, and charged mee to visite him without excuse very often.

Heeres a stirre thought I to my selfe after I was set at libertie, that is worse than an vpbrayding lesson after a britching: certainly if I had bethought mee like a rascall as I was, hee should haue had an auemarie of mee for his cynicke exhortation. God plagud mee for deriding such a graue fatherly aduertiser. List the worst throw of ill luckes.

Tracing vp and downe the City to seeke my Curtizan till the euening began to growe well in age, it fortuned, the Element as if it had dronke too much in the afternoone, powrde downe so profoundly, that I was forst to creepe like one afraid of the Watch close vnder the pentises, where the cellar doore of a Jewes house called *Zadoch* (ouer which in my direct waye I did passe) beeing vnbard on the inside, ouer head and eares I fell into it as a man falls in a ship from the oreloope into the holde: or as in an earthquake the ground should open, and a blinde man come feeling pad pad ouer the open Gulph with his staffe, should stumble on sodaine into hell. Hauing worne out the anguish of my fall a little with wallowing vp and downe, I cast vp myne eyes to see vnder what Continent I was: and loe, (O destenie) I sawe my Curtizane kissing verie louingly with a prentise. My backe and my sides I had hurt with my fall, but now my head sweld & akt worse than both. I was euen gathering winde to come vpon her with a full blast of contumely, when the Jewe (awakde with the noyse of my fall) came bustling downe the staires, and raysing his other semants, attached both the Curtizane and mee for breaking his house, and conspiring with his prentise to rob him.

It was then the lawe in *Rome*, that if anie man had a fellon falne into his hands, eyther by breaking into his house, or robbing him by the high way, hee might choose whether he would make him his bondman, or hang him. *Zadoch* (as all Jewes are couetous) casting with himselfe hee should haue no benefite by casting mee off the ladder, had another policie in his head: hee went to one Doctour *Zacharie* the popes phisition, that was a Jewe and his

Countreyman likewise, and tolde him hee had the finest bargaine for him that might bee. It is not concealed from mee (sayth he) that the time of your accustomed yearely Anatomie is at hand, which it behooues you vnder forfeiture of the foundation of your Colledge verie carefully to prouide for. The infection is great, and hardly will you get a sound bodie to deale vpon: you are my Countreyman, therefore I come to you first. Bee it knowen vnto you, I haue a young man at home falne to me for my bondman, of the age of eighteene, of stature tall, streight limm'd, of as cleere a complection as anie painters fancie can imagine: goe too, you are an honest man, and one of the scattered Children of *Abraham* you shall haue him for fiue hundred crownes. Let mee see him quoth Doctour *Zacharie*, and I will giue you as much as another. Home hee sent for mee, pinniond and shackeld I was transported alongst the streete: where passing vnder *Iulianaes* the Marques of *Mantuaes* wiues window, that was a lustie *Bona Roba* one of the popes concubines, as she had her casement halfe open, she lookt out and spide me. At the first sight she was enamored with my age and beardles face, that had in it no ill signe of phisiognomie fatall to fetters: after me shee sent to know what I was, wherein I had offended, and whether I was going? My conducts resolued them all. She hauing receiued this answere, with a lustfull collachrimation lamenting my Jewish Premunire, that bodie and goods I should lyght into the hands of such a cursed generation, inuented the meanes of my release.

But first Ile tel you what betided me after I was brought to Doctour *Zacharies*.

The purblinde Doctour put on his spectacles and lookt vppon mee: and when he had throughly viewd my face, he caused mee to bee stript naked, to feele and grope whether each lim were sound, and my skin not infected. Then hee pierst my arme to see how my bloud ranne: which assayes and searchings ended, he gaue *Zadoch* hys full price and sent him away, then lockt mee vp in a darke chamber till the day of anatomie.

O the cold sweating cares which I conceiued after I knew I should be cut like a French summer dublet. Me thought already the bloud began to gush out at my nose: if a flea on the arme had but bit me, I deemed the instrument had prickt me. Well, well, I maye scofle at a shrowde turne, but theres no such readye waye to make a man a true Christian, as to perswade himselfe he is taken vp for an anatomie. Ile depose I praid then more than I did in seauen yeare before. Not a drop of sweate trickeled downe my breast and my sides, but I dreamd it was a smooth edgde razor tenderly slicing down my breast and my sides. If any knockt at doore.

I supposed it was the beadle of Surgeons Hall come for mee. In the night I dreamd of nothing but Phlebotomie, bloudy fluxes, incamatiues, running vlcers. I durst not let out a wheale for feare through it I should bleed to death. For meate in this distance I had plum-porredge of purgations ministred mee one after another to clarifie my bloud, that it should not lye doddered in the flesh. Nor did he it so much for clarifying phisicke, as to saue charges. Miserable is that mouse that liues in a Phisitions house, *Tantalus* liues not so hunger-starud in hell, as shee doth there. Not the very crams that fall from his table, but Zachary sweepes together, and of them mouldes vp a Manna. Of the ashie parings of his bread, he would make conserue of chippings. Out of boanes after the meate was eaten off, hee would alchumize an oyle, that he sold for a shilling a dramme. His snot and spittle a hundred tymes he hath put ouer to hys Apothecarie for snowe water. Any Spider he would temper to perfect Mithridate. His rheumatique eyes when he went in the winde, or rose early in a morning, dropt as coole allom water as you would request. He was dame Niggardize sole heyre and executor.

A number of olde bookes had he eaten with the moathes and wormes, now all daye would not hee studye a dodkin, but picke those wormes and moathes out of his Librarie, and of their mixture make a preseruatiue against the plague. The licour out of his shooes he would wring to make a sacred balsamum against barrennes. Spare we him a line or two, & looke backe to *Iuliana*, who conflicted in hir thoughts about me verie debatefully, aduentured to send a messenger to Doctour *Zacharie* in her name, verie boldly to beg me of him, and if shee might not beg me, to buy me with what summes of monie soeuer he would aske. *Zacharie* iewishly and churlishly withstood both her sutes, and sayde if there were no more Christians on the earth, he would thrust his incision knife into his throate-boule immediatly. Which replie she taking at his hands most despitefully, thought to crosse him ouer the shins with as sore an ouertwhart blow yet ere a moneth to an end. The pope (I knowe not whether at her intreatie or no) within two dayes after fell sicke, Doctor *Zacharie* was sent for to minister vnto him, who seeing a little danger in his water, gaue him a gentle confortatiue for the stomack, and desired those neere about him to perswade his holynes to take some rest, and hee doubted not but he would be forthwith well. Who should receiue this mild phisicke of him but the concubine *Iuliana* his vtter enimie, shee beeing not vnprouided of strong poison at that instant, in the popes outward chamber so mingled it, that when his grande sublimitie taster came to relish it, he sunke downe starke dead on the pauement. Herewith the pope cald *Iuliana*, and askt her what strong concocted broth she had brought him. She kneeled downe on her knees, and sayd it was such as *Zacharie* the Jew had deliuered her with his owne hands, and therefore if it misliked his holines she craued pardon. The Pope without further sifting into the matter, woulde haue had *Zacharie* and all Jewes in Rome put to death, but shee hung about his knees, & with crocodile teares desired him the sentence might bee lenified, and they bee all but banisht at most. For doctor *Zacharie* quoth she, your ten times vngrateful phisition, since notwithstanding his trecherous intent, he hath much art, and many soueraigne simples, oiles, gargarismes and sirups in his closet and house that may stand your mightines in stead, I begge all his goods onely for your beatitudes preseruation and good. This request at the first was seald with a kisse, and the popes edict without delaye proclaimed throughout Rome, namely, that all foreskinne clippers whether male or female belonging to the old Jurie, should depart and auoyde vpon payne of hanging within twentie dayes after the date thereof.

Iuliana two dayes before the proclamation came out, sent her seruants to extend vppon *Zacharies* territories, his goods, his mooueables, his chattels and his seruants: who perfourmed their commission to the vtmost title, and left him not so much as master of an vrinall case or a candle boxe. It was about sixe a clocke in the euening, when those boot-halers entred: into my chamber they rusht, when I sate leaning on my elbow, and my left hand vnder my side, deuising what a kinde of death it might be to be let bloud till a man dye. I cald to minde the assertion of some Philosophers, who said the soule was nothing but bloud: then thought I, what a filthie thing were this, if I should let my soule fall and breake his necke into a bason. I had but a pimple rose with heate in that part of the veyne where they vse to pricke, and I fearfully misdeemed it was my soule searching for passage. Fie vppon it, a mans breath to bee let out a backe-doore, what a villanie it is? To dye bleeding is all one as if a man should dye pissing. Good drink makes good bloud, so that pisse is nothing but bloud vnder age. *Seneca* and *Lucan* were lobcockes to choose that death of all other: a pigge or a hogge or anie edible brute beast a cooke or a butcher deales vpon, dyes bleeding. To dye with a pricke, wherewith the faintest hearted woman vnder heauen would not be kild, O God it is infamous.

In this meditation did they seaze vpon mee, in my cloake they muffeld mee that no man might knowe mee, nor I see which waye I was carried. The first ground I toucht after I was out of *Zacharies* house, was the Countesse *Iulianaes* chamber: little did I surmise that fortune reserued mee to so faire a death. I made no other reckoning all the while they had mee on their shoulders, but that I was on horse-backe to heauen, and carried to Church on a beere, excluded for euer for drinking anie more ale or beere. *Iuliana* scornfully questioned them thus (as if I had falne into her hands beyond expectation), what proper apple-squire is this you bring so suspitiously into my chamber? what hath he done? where had you him? They aunswered likewise a farre of, that in one of *Zacharies* chambers they found him close prisoner, and thought themselues guiltie of the breach of her Ladiships commaundement if they should haue left him behinde. O quoth she, ye loue to bee double diligent, or thought peraduenture that I being a lone woman stood in neede of a loue. Bring you me a princockes beardlesse boy (I knowe not whence hee is, nor whether he would) to call my name in suspense? I tell you, you haue abused me, and I can hardly brook it at your hands. You should haue lead him to the Magistrate, no commission receiued you of me but for his goods and his seruants. They besought her to excuse their ouerweening errour, it proceeded from a zealous care of their duetie, and no negligent default But why should not I coniecture the worst quoth she? I tell you troth, I am halfe in a iealozie hee is some fantasticall amorous yonckster, who to dishonor me hath hyr'd you to this stratagem. It is a likely matter that such a man as *Zacharie* should make a prison of his house, and deale in matters of state. By your leaue sir gallant, vnder locke and key shal you stay with me, till I haue enquirde further of you, you shall be sifted thoroughly ere you and I part Goe maide shew him to the further chamber at the ende of the gallerie that lookes into the garden: you my trim pandars I pray garde him thether as you tooke paines to bring him hether. When you haue so done, see the dores be made fast, and come your way. Heere was a wily wench had her liripoop without book, she was not to seeke in her knackes and shifts: such are all women, not one of them but hath a cloak for the raine, and can bleare her husbands eyes as she list. Not too much of this madam Marques at once: wele step a little backe, and dilate what *Zadoch* the Jew did with my curtizan, after he had sold me to *Zacharie*. Of an ill tree I hope you are not so ill sighted in grafting to expect good frute: he was a Jew, & intreated her like a Jew. Under shadow of enforcing her to tell how much money she had of his prentice so to bee trayned to his cellar, hee stript her, and scourgd her from top to toe tantara. Day by day hee disgested his meate with leading her the measures. A diamond Delphinicall drye leachour it was.

The ballet of the whipper of late dayes here in England, was but a scoffe in comparison of him. All the colliers of Romford, who hold their corporation by yarking the blind beare at Paris garden, were but bunglers to him, he had the right agility of the lash, there were none of them could made the cord come aloft with a twange halfe like him. Marke the ending, marke the ending. The tribe of Juda is adiudged from Rome to bee trudging, they may no longer be lodged there, all the Albumazers, Rabisacks, Gedeons, Tebiths, Benhadads, Benrodans, Zedechiahs, Halies of them were banquerouts and turnd out of house and home. *Zacharie* came running to *Zadochs* in sack cloth and ashes presently after his goods were confiscated and tolde him how he was serued, and what decree was comming out against them all. Descriptions stand by, heere is to be expressed the furie of Lucifer when he was turnd ouer heauen barre for a wrangler. There is a toad fish, which taken out of the water swels more than one would thinke his skin could holde, and bursts in his face that toucheth him. So swelled *Zadoch*, and was readie to burst out of his skinne, and shoote his bowels like chaine-shot full at *Zacharies* face for bringing him such balefull tidings, his eies glared and burnt bliewe like brimstone and *aqua vito* set on fire in an egshell, his verie nose lightned glow-wormes, his teeth crasht and grated together, like the ioynts of a high building cracking and rocking like a cradle, when as a tempest takes her full but against his broad side. He swore, he curst, and said, these be they that worshippe that crucifide God of Nazareth, heres the fruits of their newfound gospell, sulphur and gunpouder carry them all quick to Gehenna. I would spend my soule willingly, to haue this triple headed Pope with all his sin-absoued whores, and oile-greased priests borne with a blacke sant on the deuills backes in procession to the pit of perdition. Would I might sinke presently into ye earth, so I might blow vp this Rome, this whore of *Babylon* into the aire with my breath. If I must be banisht, if those heathen dogs will needes rob me of my goods, I wyll poyson their springs and conduit heades, whence they receiue all their water round about the citie, He tice all the yong children into my house that I can get, and cutting their throates barrell them vp in poudring beefe tubbes, and so send them to victuall the popes galleyes. Ere the officers come to extend, Ile bestowe a hundred pound on a doale of bread, which Ile cause to bee kneaded with Scorpions oy le that may kill more than the plague. Ile hire them that make their wafers or sacramentarie gods to minge them after the same sort, so in the zeale of their superstitious religion, shall they languish and droup like carrion. If there be euer a blasphemous coniurer, that can call the windes from their brazen caues, and make the cloudes trauell before their time, Ile giue him the other hundred pounds to disturbe the heauens a whole weeke together with thunder and lightning, if it bee for nothing but to sowre all the wines in *Rome*, and turne them to vinegar. As long as they haue either oyle or wine, this plague feedes but pinglingly vpon them.

Zadoch, Zadoch said Doctor *Zacharie*, (cutting him off) thou threatenest the aire, whiles wee perish heere on earth. It is the Countesse *Iuliana* the Marquesse of*Mantuaes* wife and no other, that hath complotted our confusion. Aske not how, but insist in my words, and assist in reuenge.

As how, as how, said *Zadoch*, shrugging and shrubbing. More happie than the Patriarches were I, if crusht to death with the greatest torments *Romes* tyrants haue tride, there might be quintessenst out of me one quart of precious poyson. I haue a leg with an issue, shall I cut it off, and from his fount of corruption extract a venome worse than anie serpents? If thou wilt, Ile goe to a house that is infected, where catching the plague, and hauing got a running sore vpon me, Ile come and deliuer her a supplication, and breathe vpon her. I know my breath stinkes so alreadie, that it is within halfe a degree of poyson. Ile pay her home if I perfect it with any more putrifaction.

No, no brother *Zadoch* answered *Zacharie*, that is not the way. Canst thou prouide mee ere a bondmaide, indued with singular & diuine qualified beautie, whome as a present from our synagogue thou maist commend vnto her, desiring her to be good and gracious vnto vs.

I haue, I am for you quoth *Zadoch: Diamante* come forth. Heeres a wench (said he) of as cleare a skin as *Susanna*, shee hath not a wemme on her flesh from the soale of the foote to the crowne of the head: how thinke you master doctor, will shee not serue the turne?

She will, said *Zacharie:* and therefore Ile tell you what charge I would haue committed to her. But I care not if I disclose it onely to her. Maid, (if thou beest a maid) come hether to mee, thou must be sent to the countesse of *Mantuaes* about a small peece of seruice, whereby being now a bond woman thou shalt purchase freedome, and gaine a large dowrie to thy marriage. I know thy master loues thee derely though hee will not let thee perceiue so much, hee intends after hee is dead to make thee his heire, for he hath no children: please him in that I shall instruct thee, and thou art made for euer. So it is, that the pope is farre out of liking with the countesse of *Mantua* his concubine, and hath put his trust in me his phisition to haue her quietly and charitably made away. Now I cannot intend it, for I haue manie cures in hand which call vpon me hourely: thou if thou beest plac'd with her as her waiting maid or cup-bearer, maist temper poyson with her broth, her meate, her drinke, her oyles, her sirrups, and neuer bee bewraid. I will not say whether the pope hath heard of thee, and thou maist come to bee his lemman in her place, if thou behaue thy selfe wisely. What, hast thou the heart to go thorough with it or no? *Diamante* deliberating with her selfe in what hellish seruitude she liu'd with the Jew, and that she had no likelihood to be releast of it, but fall from euill to worse if she omitted this opportunitie, resigned her selfe ouer wholly to be disposed and emploid as seemed best vnto them. Therevpon, without further consultation, her wardrop was richly rigd, her tongue smooth fil'd & new edg'd on the whetstone, her drugs deliuerd her, and presented she was by *Zadoch* her master to the countesse, together with some other slight new-fangles, as from the whole congregation, desiring her to stand their merciful mistresse, and sollicite the Pope for them, that through one mans ignorant offence were all generally in disgrace with him, and had incurred the cruell sentence of losse of goods and of banishment.

Iuliana liking wel the pretie round face of my black browe *Diamante*, gaue the Jew better countenance than otherwise she would haue done, and told him for her owne part shee was but a priuate woman, and could promise nothing confidently of his holines: for though he had suffred himselfe to bee ouerruled by her in some humors, yet in this that tutcht him so nerely, she knew not how he would be enclind: but what lay in her either to pacifie or perswade him they should be sure of, and so crau'd his absence.

His backe turnd, shee askt *Diamante* what countrey woman she was, what frends she had, and how she fell into the hands of that Jew? She answered, that she was a *Magnificoes* daughter of *Venice*, stolne when she was yong from her frends, and sold to this Jew for a bondwoman, who (quoth she) hath vsde me so iewishly and tyrannously, that for euer I must celebrate the memorie of this day, wherein I am deliuered from his Jurisdiction. Alas (quoth she deep sighing) why did I enter into anie mention of my owne misusage? It will be thought that that which I am now to reueale, proceeds of mallice not truth. Madam, your life is sought by these Jewes that sue to you. Blush not, nor be troubled in your minde, for with warning I shall arme you against all their intentions. Thus and thus (quoth she) said doctor *Zacharie* vnto me, this poyson he deliuered me. Before I was cald in to them, such and such consultation through the creuise of the dore fast lockt did I heare betwixt them. Denie it if they can, I will iustifie it: onely I beseech you to be fauorable Ladie vnto me, and let me not fall againe into the hands of those vipers.

Iuliana said little but thought vnhappely, onely she thankt her for detecting it, and vowed though she were her bond woman to be a mother vnto her. The poyson she tooke of her, and set it vp charily on a shelfe in her closet, thinking to keepe it for some good purposes: as for example, when I was consumed and worne to the bones through her abuse, she would giue me but a dram too much, and pop mee into a priuie. So shee had seru'd some of her paramours ere that, and if God had not sent *Diamante* to be my redeemer, vndoubtedly I had drunke of the same cup.

In a leafe or two before was I lockt vp: heere in this page the foresaid goodwife Countesse comes to me, shee is no longer a iudge but a client. How she came, in what manner of attyre, with what immodest and vncomely words shee courted me, if I should take vpon me to enlarge, all modest eares would abhorre me. Some inconuenience she brought me too by her harlot-like behauiour, of which inough I can neuer repent me.

Let that bee forgiu'n and forgotten, fleshly delights could not make her slothfull or slumbring in reuenge against *Zadoch*. Shee set men about him to incense and egge him on in courses of discontentment, and other supervising espialls, to plye followe and spurre for-warde those suborning incensers. Both which playd their parts so, that *Zadoch* of his own nature violent, swore by the arke of *Iehoua* to set the whole citie on fire ere he went out of it. *Zacharie* after he had furnisht the wench with the poyson, and giu'n her instructions to goe to the diuell, durst not staye one houre for feare of disclosing, but fled to the Duke of *Burbon* that after sackt Rome, & there practised with his bastardship all the mischief against the pope and *Rome* that enuie could put into his minde. *Zadoch* was left behinde for the hangman. According to his oath, he prouided balls of wilde fire in a readines, and laid traines of gunpouder in a hundred seuerall places of the citie to blow it vp, which hee had set fire too, as also bandied his balls abroad, if his attendant spies had not taken him with ye manner. To the straightest prison in *Rome* he was dragged, where from top to toe he was clogd with fetters and manacles. *Iuliana* informed the pope of *Zacharies* and his practise, *Zachary* was sought for, but *non est inuentus*, he was packing long before. Commaundement was giu'n, that *Zadoch* whom they had vnder hand and seale of locke and key, should be executed with all the fiery torments that could be found out.

He make short worke, for I am sure I haue wearied all my readers. To the execution place was he brought, where first and formost he was stript, then on a sharpe yron stake fastened in the ground, had he his fundament pitcht, which stake ran vp along into his bodie like a spit, vnder his arme-hoales two of like sort, a great bonfire they made round about him, wherewith his flesh rosted not burnd: and euer as with the heate his skinne blistered, the fire was drawne aside, and they basted him with a mixture of Aqua fortis, allam water, and Mercury sublimatum, which smarted to the very soule of him, and searcht him to the marrowe. Then did they scourge hys backe parts so blistered and basted, with burning whips of red hot wire: his head they noynted ouer with pitch and tarre, and so enflamed it. To his priuie members they tied streaming fierworkes, the skinne from the crest of his shoulder, as also from his elbowes, his huckle bones, his knees, his ankles they pluckt and gnawd off with sparkling pincers: hys breast and his belly with seale skins they grated ouer, which as fast as they grated & rawed, one stoode ouer and lau'd with smithes cindry water and *aqua vito*: his nayles they halfe raised vp, and then vnderpropt them with Sharpe prickes like a taylers shop windowe halfe open on a holiday: euerie one of his fingers they rent vp to the wrist: his toes they brake off by the rootes, and let them still hang by a little skinne. In conclusion, they had a small oyle fire, such as men blow light bubbles of glasse with, and beginning at his feet, they let him lingringly burne vp limme by limme, till his hart was consumed, and then he died. Triumph women, this was the end of the whipping Jew, contriued by a woman, in reuenge of two women, her selfe and her maid.

I haue told you or should tell you in what credit *Diamante* grew with her mistres. *Iuliana* neuer dreamed but she was an authenticall maide: she made her the chiefe of her bed chamber, she appointed none but her to looke into me, and serue me of such necessaries as I lacked. You must suppose when wee met there was no small reioycing on either part, much like the three Brothers that went three seuerall wayes to seeke their fortunes, and at the yeres end at those three crosse waies met againe, and told one another how they sped: so after we had been long asunder seeking our fortunes, wee commented one to another most kindly, what crosse haps had encountred vs. Nere a six houres but the Countesse cloyd mee with her companie. It grew to this passe, that either I must finde out some miraculous meanes of escape, or drop away in a consumption, as one pin'd for lacke of meate: I was cleane spent and done, there was no hope of me.

The yere held on his course to domes day, when Saint *Peters* day dawned. That day is a day of supreme solemnitie in *Rome*, when the Embassador of *Spaine* comes and presents a milke white iennet to the pope, that kneeles downe vppon his owne accord in token of obeisaunce and humilitie before him, and lets him stride on his backe as easie as one strides ouer a blocke: with this iennet is offered a rich purse of a yard length, full of Peter-pence. No musique that hath the gift of vtterance, but sounds all the while: coapes and costly vestments decke the hoarsest and beggerliest singing man, not a clarke or sexten is absent, no nor a mule nor a foote-cloth belonging to anie cardinall, but attends on the taile of the triumph. The pope himselfe is borne in his pontificalibus thorough the *Burgo* (which is the cheefe streete in *Rome*) to the Embassadors house to dinner, and thether resorts all the assembly: where if a Poet should spend all his life time in describing a banquet, he could not feast his auditors halfe so wel with words, as he doth his guests with iunkets.

To this feast *Iuliana* addressed her selfe like an Angell: in a littour of greene needle-worke wrought like an arbor, and open on euerie side was she borne by foure men, hidden vnder cloth rough plushed and wouen like eglantine and wood-bine. At the foure corners it was topt with foure round christall cages of Nightingales. For foote men, on either side of her went foure virgins clad in lawne, with lutes in their hands playing. Next before her two and two in order, a hundred pages in sutes of white cipresse, and long horsemens coates of cloth of siluer: who being all in white, aduanced euery one of them her picture, enclosed in a white round screene of feathers, such as is carried ouer great Princesses heads when they ride in summer, to keepe them from the heate of the sun. Before the went a foure-score bead women she maintain'd in greene gownes, scattring strowing hearbs and floures, After her followed the blinde, the halt and the lame sumptuously apparailed like Lords: and thus past she on to Saint *Peters*.

Interea quid agitur donti, how ist at home all this while. My curtizan is left my keeper, the keyes are committed vnto her, she is mistres *fac totunt*. Against our countesse we conspire, packe vp all her iewels, plate, money that was extant, and to the water side send them: to conclude, couragiously rob her, and run away. *Quid non auri sacra fames?* What defame will not golde salue. Hee mistooke himself that inuented the prouerbe, *Dimicandum est pro aris & fama*: for it should haue been *pro auro & fama*: not for altares and fires we must contend, but for gold and fame.

Oares nor winde could not stirre nor blow faster, than we toyld out of *Tiber*; a number of good fellowes would giue size ace and the dice that with as little toyle they could leaue Tyburne behinde them. Out of ken we were ere the Countesse came from the feast When she returned and found her house not so much pestred as it was wont, her chests her closets and her cupbords broke open to take aire, and that both I and my keeper was missing: O then shee fared like a franticke Bacchinall, she stampt, she star'd, shee beate her head against the walls, scratcht her face, bit her fingers, and strewd all the chamber with her haire. None of her seuants durst stay in her sight, but she beate them out in heapes, and bad them goe seeke search they knew not where, and hang themselues, and neuer looke her in the face more, if they did not hunt vs out. After her furie had reasonably spent it selfe, her breast began to swell with the mother, caused by her former fretting & chafing, and she grew verie ill at ease. Whereuppon shee knockt for one of her maids, and had her run into her closet, and fetch her a little glasse that stood on the vpper shelfe, wherein there was *spiritus vini*. The maid went, & mistaking tooke the glasse of poyson which *Diamante* had giu'n her, and she kept in store for me. Comming with it as fast as her legs could carrie her, her mistres at her returne was in a swound, and lay for dead on the floore, wherat she shrikt out, and fel a rubbing & chafing her very busily. When that would not serue, she tooke a keye and opened her mouth, and hauing heard that *spiritus vini* was a thing of mightie operation, able to call a man from death to life, shee tooke the poyson, and verely thinking it to be *spiritus vini* (such as she was sent for) powrd a large quantitie of it into her throate, and iogd on her backe to disgest it. It reuiu'd her with a merrie vengeance, for it kilde her outright: only she awakend and lift vp her hands, but spake nere a word. Then was the maid in her grandames beanes, and knew not what should become of her: I heard the Pope tooke pitie on her, and because her trespasse was not voluntary but chancemedly, he assigned her no other punishment but this, to drinke out the rest of the poyson in the glasse that was left, and so goe scot-free. We carelesse of these mischances, helde on our flight, and saw no man come after vs but we thought had pursued vs. A theefe they say mistakes euerie bush for a true man, thewinde ratled not in anie bush by the way as I rode, but I straight drew my rapier. To *Bolognia* with a merrie gale wee posted, where wee lodged our selues in a blinde streete out of the way, and kept secret manie dayes: but when we perceiued we saild in the hauen, that the winde was layd, and no alarum made after vs, we boldly came abroad: & one day hearing of a more desperat murdrer than *Cayn* that was to be executed, we followed the multitude, and grutcht not to lend him our eyes at his last parting.

Who should it bee but one *Cutwolfe*, a wearish dwarfish writhen fac'd cobler, brother to *Bartoll* the Italian, that was confederate with *Esdras* of *Granado*, and at that time stole away my curtizan, when he rauisht *Heraclide*.

It is not so naturall for me to epitomize his impietie, as to heare him in his owne person speake vppon the wheele where he was to suffer.

Prepare your eares and your teares, for neuer till this thrust I anie tragicall matter vpon you. Strange and wonderfull are Gods iudgements, heere shine they in their glory. Chast *Heraclide* thy bloud is laid vp in heauens treasurie, not one drop of it was lost, but lent out to vsurie: water powred forth sinkes downe quietly into the earth, but bloud spilt on the ground sprinkles vp to the firmament. Murder is wide-mouthd, and will not let God rest till he grant reuenge. Not onely the bloud of the slaughtred innocent but the soule ascendeth to his throne, and there cries out & exclaimes for iustice and recompence. Guiltles soules that liue euerie houre subiect to violence, and with your despairing feares doo much empaire Gods prouidence: fasten your eyes on this spectacle that will adde to your faith. Referre all your oppressions afflictions and iniuries to the euen ballanced eye of the Almightie, hee it is, that when your patience sleepeth, will bee most exceeding mindfull of you.

This is but a glose vpon the text: thus *Cutwolfe* begins his insulting oration.

Men and people that haue made holy-daie to behold my pained flesh toile on the wheele. Expect not of me a whining penitent slaue, that shal do nothing but crie and saie his praiers, and so be crusht in peeces. My bodie is little, but my minde is as great as a Giants: the soule which is in mee, is the verie soul of *Iulius Cosar* by reuersion. My name is *Cutwolfe*, neither better nor worse by occupation, than a poore cobler of *Verona*, coblers are men and kings are no more. The occasion of my comming hether at this present, is to haue a fewe of my bones broken (as we are all borne to die) for being the death of the Emperour of homicides *Esdras of Granado*. About two yeares since in the streetes of *Rome* he slew the onely and eldest brother I had named *Bartoll*, in quarrelling about a curtizan. The newes brought to me as I was sitting in my shop vnder a stall knocking in of tackes, I think I raisd vp my bristles, solde pritchaule, spunge, blacking tub, and punching yron, bought mee rapier and pistoll, and to goe I went. Twentie months together I pursued him, from *Rome to Naples, from Naples to Caiete passing ouer the riuer, from Caiete to Syenna, from Syenna to Florence, from Florence to Parma, from Parma to Pauia, from Pauia to Syon, from Syon to Geneua, from Geneua backe againe towards Rome*: where in the way it was my chance to meet him in the nicke here at *Bolognia*, as I will tell you how. I saw a great fray in the streetes as I past along, and manie swords walking, wherevpon drawing neerer, and enquiring who they were, answer was returned mee it was that notable Bandetto *Esdras of Granado*. O so I was tickled in the spleene with that word, my heart hopt & daunst, my elbowes itcht, my fingers friskt, I wist not what should become of my feete, nor knew what I did for ioy. The fray parted. I thought it not conuenient to single him out (being a sturdie knaue) in the street, but to stay till I had got him at more aduantage. To his lodging I dogd him, lay at the dore all night where hee entred, for feare hee should giue me the slip anie way. Betimes in the morning I rung the bell and crau'd to speake with him: vp to his chamber dore I was brought, where knocking, hee rose in his shirt and let me in, and when I was entred, bad me lock the dore and declare my arrant, and so he slipt to bed againe.

Marrie this quoth I is my arrant Thy name is *Esdras of Granado*, is it not? Most treacherously thou slewst my brother *Bartoll* about two yeres agoe in the streetes of *Rome*: his death am I come to reuenge. In quest of thee euer since aboue three thousand miles haue I trauaild. I haue begd to maintaine me the better part of the waye, onely because I would intermit no time from my pursute in going backe for monie. Now haue I got thee naked in my power, die thou shalt, though my mother and my grandmother dying did intreate for thee. I haue promist the diuell thy soule within this houre, breake my word I will not, in thy breast I intend to burie a bullet. Stirre not, quinch not, make no noyse: for if thou dost it will be worse for thee. Quoth *Esdras*, what euer thou bee at whose mercie I lye, spare me, and I wil giue thee as much gold as thou wilt aske. Put me to anie paines my life reserued, and I willingly will sustaine them: cut off my armes and legs, and leaue me as a lazer to some loathsome spittle, where I may but liue a yeare to pray and repent me. For thy brothers death the despayre of minde that hath euer since haunted mee, the guiltie gnawing worme of conscience I feele may bee sufficient penaunce. Thou canst not send me to such a hell, as alreadie there is in my hart. To dispatch me presently is no reuenge, it wil soone be forgotten: let me dye a lingring death, it will be remembred a great deale longer. A lingring death maye auaile my soule, but it is the illest of ills that can befortune my bodie. For my soules health I beg my bodies torment: bee not thou a diuell to torment my soule, and send me to eternall damnation. Thy ouer-hanging sword hides heauen from my sight, I dare not looke vp, least I embrace my deaths-wound vnawares: I cannot pray to God, and plead to thee both at once. Ay mee, alreadie I see my life buried in the wrinckles of thy browes: say but I shall liue, though thou meanest to kill me. Nothing confounds like to suddaine terror, it thrusts euerie sense out of office. Poyson wrapt vp in sugred pills is but halfe a poyson: the feare of deaths lookes are more terrible than his stroake. The whilest I viewe death, my faith is deaded: where a mans feare is, there his heart is. Feare neuer engenders hope: how can I hope that heauens father will saue mee from the hell euerlasting, when he giues me ouer to the hell of thy furie.

Heraclide, now thinke I on thy teares sowen in the dust (thy teares, that my bloudie minde made barraine). In reuenge of thee, God hardens this mans heart against mee: yet I did not slaughter thee, though hundreds else my hand hath brought to the shambles. Gentle sir, learne of mee what it is to clog your conscience with murder, to haue your dreames, your sleepes, your solitarie walkes troubled and disquieted with murther. Your shaddowe by daye will affright you, you will not see a weapon vnsheathd, but immediately you will imagine it is predestinate for your destruction.

This murder is a house diuided within it selfe: it subornes a mans owne soule to informe against him: his soule (being his accuser) brings foorth his two eyes as witnesses agaynst him: and the least eye witnesse is vnrefutable. Plucke out my eyes if thou wilt, and depriue my trayterous soule of her two best witnesses. Digge out my blasphemous tongue with thy dagger, both tongue and eyes will I gladly forgoe, to haue a little more time to thinke on my iourney to heauen.

Deferre a while thy resolution. I am not at peace with the world, for euen but yesterdaye I fought, and in my furie threatened further vengeaunce: had I face to face askt forgiuenesse, I should thinke halfe my sinnes were forgiuen. A hundred Diuells haunt mee daily for my horrible murders: the diuells when I dye will be loath to goe to hell with mee, for they desir'd of Christ he would not send them to hell before their time; if they goe not to hell, into thee they will goe, and hideously vexe thee for turning them out of their habitation. Wounds I contemne, life I prize light, it is another worlds tranquilitie which makes me so timerous: euerlasting damnation, euerlasting howling and lamentation. It is not from death I request thee to deliuer me, but from this terror of torments eternitie. Thy brothers bodie onely I pierst vnaduisedly, his soule meant I no harme too at all: my bodie & soule both shalt thou cast awaye quite, if thou doost at this instant what thou maist Spare me, spare me I beseech thee: by thy owne soules saluation I desire thee, seeke not my soules vtter perdition: in destroying me, thou destroyest thy selfe and me.

Eagerly I replide after his long suppliant oration; Though I knewe God would neuer haue mercie on mee except I had mercie on thee, yet of thee no mercie would I haue. Reuenge in our tragedies continually is raised from hell: of hell doo I esteeme better than heauen, if it affoord me reuenge. There is no heauen but reuenge. I tell thee, I would not haue vndertooke so much toyle to gaine heauen, as I haue done in pursuing thee for reuenge. Diuine reuenge, of which (as of the ioyes aboue) there is no fulnes or satietie.

Looke how my feete are blistered with following thee from place to place. I haue riuen my throat withouerstraining it to curse thee. I haue grownd my teeth to pouder with grating and grinding them together for anger, when anie hath nam'd thee. My tongue with vaine threates is bolne, and waxen too big for my mouth. My eies haue broken their strings with staring and looking ghastly, as I stood deuising how to frame or set my countenance when I met thee. I haue nere spent my strength in imaginarie acting on stone wals, what I determined to execute on thee. Entreate not, a miracle maye not repriue thee: villaine, thus march I with my blade into thy bowels.

Stay, stay exclaimed *Esdras*, and heare mee but one word further. Though neither for God nor man thou carest, but placeth thy whole felicitie in murder, yet of thy felicitie learne how to make a greater felicitie. Respite me a little from thy swords poynt, and set mee about some execrable enterprise, that may subuert the whole state of Christendome, and make all mens eares tingle that heare of it. Commaund me to cut all my kindreds throates, to burne men women and children in their beds in millions, by firing their Cities at midnight. Be it Pope, Emperour or Turke that displeaseth thee, he shal not breath on the earth. For thy sake will I sweare and forsweare, renounce my baptisme, and all the interest I haue in any other sacrament. Onely let me liue how miserable soeuer, be it in a dungeon amongst toades, serpents and adders, or set vp to the necke in dung. No paines I will refuse how euer proroged, to haue a little respite to purifie my spirit: oh heare me, heare me, and thou canst not be hardned against me.

At this his importunitie paused a little, not as retyring from my wreakful resolution, but going back to gather more forces of vengeance. With my selfe I deuised how to plague him double for his base minde. My thoughts traueld in quest of some notable newe Italionisme, whose murdrous platforme might not onely extend on his bodie, but his soule also. The ground worke of it was this. That whereas he had promised for my sake to sweare and forsweare, and commit *Iulian*-like violence on the highest seales of religion· if he would but thus farre satisfie me he should bee dismist from my furie. First and formost he should renounce God and his lawes, and vtterly disclaime the whole title or interest he had in anie couenaunt of saluation. Next he should curse him to his face, as *Iob* was willed by his wife, and write an absolute firme obligation of his soule to the diuell, without condition or exception. Thirdly and lastly (hauing done this), hee should praye to God feruently neuer to haue mercie vppon him, or pardon him. Scarce had I propounded these articles vnto him, but he was beginning his blasphemous abiurations. I wonder the earth opened not and swallowed vs both hearing the bold tearmes he blasted forth in contempt of Christianitie: Heauen hath thundred when halfe lesse contumelies against it haue been vttered. Able they were to raise Saints and Martirs from their graues, and plucke Christ himselfe from the right hand of his father. My ioints trembled & quakt with attending them, my haire stood vpright, & my hart was turned wholly to fire. So affectionately and zealously did hee giue himselfe ouer to infidelitie, as if sathan had gotten the vpper hand of our high Maker. The veyne in his left hand that is deriued from his heart with no faint blow he pierst, & with the bloud that flowd from it, writ a ful obligation of his soule to the diuell: yea, more earnestly he praid vnto God neuer to forgiue it his soule, than manie Christians doo to saue theyr soules. These fearfull ceremonies brought to an end, I bad him ope his mouth and gape wide. He did so (as what wil not slaues doo for feare). Therwith made I no more adoo, but shot him ful into the throat with my pistol: no more spake he after, so did I shoote him that hee might neuer speak after, or repent him.

His body being dead lookd as blacke as a toad: the diuell presently branded it for his owne. This is the fault that hath called me hether. No true *Italian* but will honor me for it Reuenge is the glory of Armes, and the highest performance of valure: reuenge is whatsoeuer wee call law or iustice. The farther we wade in reuenge, the nerer come we to the throne of the Almightie. To his scepter it is properly ascribed, his scepter he lends vnto man, when he lets one man scourge another. All true *Italians* imitate mee, in reuenging constantly, and dying valiantly. Hangman to thy taske, for I am readie for the vtmost of thy rigor. Herewith all the people (outragiously incensed) with one conioyned outcrye yelled mainely, Away with him, away with him, Executioner torture him, teare him, or we will teare thee in peeces if thou spare him.

The executioner needed no exhortation herevnto, for of his owne nature was he hackster good enough: olde excellent hee was at a bone-ache. At the first chop with his wood-knife would he fish for a mans heart, and fetch it out as easily as a plum from the bottome of a porredge pot. Hee would cracke neckes as fast as a cooke crackes egges: a fidler cannot turne his pin so soone, as he would turn a man of the ladder. Brauely did hee drum on this *Cutwolfes* bones, not breaking them outright, but like a sadler knocking in of tackes, iarring on them quaueringly with his hammer a great while together. No ioynt about him but with a hatchet he had for the nonce, he disioynted halfe, and then with boyling lead souldred vp the wounds from bleeding. His tongue he puld out, least he should blaspheme in his torment: venomous stinging wormes hee thrust into his eares, to keep his head rauingly occupied: with cankers scruzed to peeces hee rubd his mouth and his gums. No lim of his but was lingringly splinterd in shiuers. In this horror left they him on the wheele as in hel: where yet liuing, hee might behold his flesh legacied amongst the foules of the aire. Unsearchable is the booke of our destenies. One murder begetteth another: was neuer yet bloud-shed barrain from the beginning of the world to this day. Mortifiedly abiected and danted was I with this truculent tragedie of *Cutwolfe* and *Esdras*. To such straight life did it thence forward incite me, that ere I went out of *Bolognia* I married my curtizane, performed manie aimes deedes; and hasted so fast out of the *Sodom* of *Italy*, that within fortie daies I arriued at the King of *Englands* Campe twixt *Ardes* and *Guines* in *France*: where he with great triumphes met and entertained the Emperour and the French King, and feasted manie dayes. And so as my Storie began with the King at *Turnay* and *Turwin*, I thinke meete heere to end it with the King at *Ardes & Guines*. All the conclusiue Epilogue I will make is this; that if herein I haue pleased any, it shall animate me to more paynes in this kinde. Otherwise I will sweare vpon an English Chronicle, neuer to bee outlandish Chronicler more while I liue. Farewell as manie as wish me well. *Iune* 27. 1593.

Finis.

Chiswick Press:—Charles Whittingham And Co., Tooks Court, Chancery Lane.

Made in the USA
Columbia, SC
26 September 2019